VANISHING
ISLANDS

A Story of History's "Invisible People" on Islands in the Chesapeake Bay

How They Lived and Worked and Played

by

Frances Kolarek

HERITAGE BOOKS
2008

HERITAGE BOOKS

AN IMPRINT OF HERITAGE BOOKS, INC.

Books, CDs, and more—Worldwide

For our listing of thousands of titles see our website
at
www.HeritageBooks.com

Published 2008 by
HERITAGE BOOKS, INC.
Publishing Division
100 Railroad Ave. #104
Westminster, Maryland 21157

International Standard Book Numbers
Paperbound: 978-0-7884-4901-7
Clothbound: 978-0-7884-7502-3

To Mary,

For whom The House was home.

Table of Contents

List of Illustrations

Acknowledgments

Had it not been for John S. McCann's encouragement, this book would never have been written or submitted for publication. During a course he taught in autobiographical writing he encouraged me, read the manuscript, edited it, and nudged me to find a publisher for it.

Friend and computer maven Leeann Steuer set my feet down the right path in formatting the book as I made a grudging transition from Macintosh to Word. Patient, helpful, tactful.

The drawings, which add so much, were a gift from the late Eric Dennard, an artist who moved to Taylor's Island to work.

And author and friend Faith Jackson has cheered me on all the while.

I thank them all.

Of the Chesapeake Bay area, Captain John Smith wrote in 1612:

"...heaven and earth never agreed better to frame a place for man's habitation..."

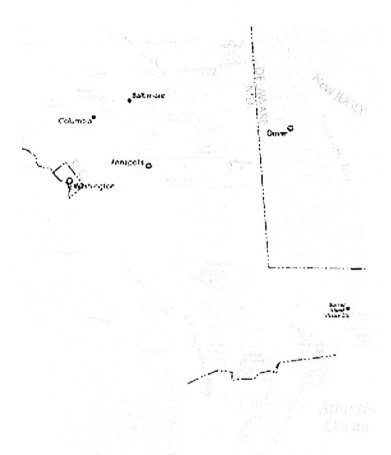

Maryland's Chesapeake Bay Area

Poplar Island

Poplar Island once belonged to Charles Carroll, grandson of one of the signers of the Declaration of Independence. Mr. Carroll had heard from seamen who had sailed around Cape Horn and on to the Far East, that black cat pelts were regarded as a universal panacea in China. He got an idea. Why not bring black cats to Poplar Island where they would breed and produce black cats which would produce even more black cats? The export of their pelts to the vast China market would provide a profitable business.

His agent advertised in the *Easton Gazette* of December, 1847 offering to pay 25 cents each for female black cats delivered to Poplar Island or to his store. The tomcats were already in place and the females were taken to the island to fatten off a diet of fish, of which there was aplenty, and produce litters of black kittens. Carroll must have sat back and thought: How can I lose?

Here's how: a hard freeze descended on the Chesapeake Bay forming an ice bridge between the Island and the mainland and the cats took off, heading for the warmth and comfort of their former homes. The venture came to naught. For the cats, a happy ending. For Poplar Island itself, the story takes a different turn.

It's gone.

It once lay off Talbot County on the Eastern Shore of Mary-land. The term Del-Mar-Va peninsula describes the isthmus that separates the Chesapeake Bay from the Atlantic Ocean and is made up of parts of Delaware, Maryland and Virginia. That part of Maryland that lies on this peninsula is known as the Eastern Shore of Maryland. Here, the term "mainland" refers to the Eastern Shore.

Some 13 islands in the Bay have disappeared entirely since the region was first mapped,[1] leaving behind no record of the people who once lived on them or their history. And once an

---

[1] The University of Maryland's Laboratory for Coastal Research

island is gone, its history and its heritage disappear along with it.

"A lot of history has been lost," Michael S. Kearney of the University of Maryland, says.[2] "Some of these islands were plantations. We tried to find an old graveyard that was marked on survey maps of James Island as late as the 1930s. Apparently it's gone in the drink."

Poplar Island, said to have consisted of some 1,000 acres when John Smith sailed up the Chesapeake Bay in 1608, is a prime example of an island's struggle to hold its head above water. Called either Popeley's or Poplin depending on your source, it came to be known simply as Poplar Island. By the end of the twentieth century there were three scant fragments left of a place that once played host to Presidents Franklin D. Roosevelt and Harry Truman.

2 The Case of the Vanishing Islands, National Geographic, April 28, 2000

Sharp's Island

Sharp's Island lies south of Poplar Island at the mouth of the Little Choptank River. Its lighthouse leans crazily as if it were imitating the tower in Pisa. In 1977 heavy ice floes rammed its base and knocked it off balance. The Bay never quits. Winter and summer, it wars with the land. When the present lighthouse was built -- it's the third one to occupy Sharp's Island -- there was still some land around its base. Within a few years none of it was left. During the 19th century the island shrank down to a nubbin, although it had once been home to a number of families. There's not a lot about this place on record. Just another among the 13 vanished islands.

The Coast Guard is facing a hard decision about whether to keep the present structure -- they have to maintain it or do away with it. Preservationists rally to defense of the lighthouse.

There is agreement that a light is needed at the Sharp's Island location to warn shipping of the shoals south of Poplar Island at the mouth of the Little Choptank River.

If it were not for the lighthouse there'd be nothing left to speak of.

3

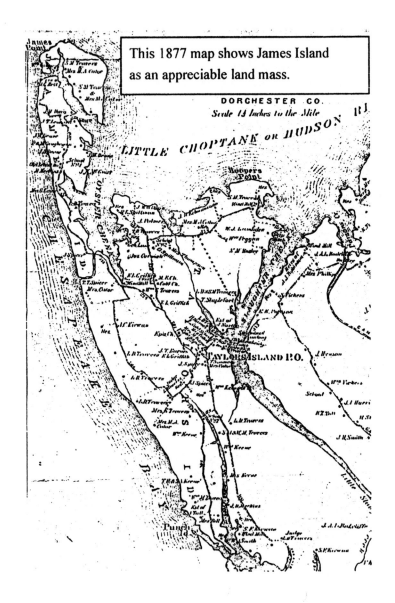

This 1877 map shows James Island as an appreciable land mass.

DORCHESTER CO.
Scale 1.4 Inches to the Mile

James Island

As early as 1662 a 400-acre farm called Armstrong's Hogpen stood on Saint James Island, a promontory just north of Taylor's Island. It was washed on its eastern shores by the Little Choptank River, on the West by the Chesapeake Bay and it was vulnerable to attack by water and, during the Revolution, by the British. Marauding forces looking for provender found plenty there. The record shows that William Geohegan, among other islanders, swore that "property was taken away from his home on James Point on St. James Island by the British" and was paid 8 pounds 17 shillings in recompense by the fledgling United States government in 1785.

The years rolled by and James Island looked to many like a good place to put down roots, raise a family and prosper. In 1803 Thomas Navy's hopes ran so high that he paid John Woolford 53 pounds 10 shillings for a 95-acre plot.

By mid-century some 200 men, women and children had settled into homes. They built a church, set up a store and organized a school. A former pupil named Clara Walker, reminiscing many years later, remembered a "big old cast-iron stove" that kept the one-room school house warm in winter. And her mind reached back to Tom Leonard, the parsimonious storekeeper, who once, believe it or not, broke a gingersnap in half to make even weight! "He never gave too little; but he never gave too much either," said Clara.

The Sunday school picnics at the Methodist Church lived in her memory.

"Cakes and cakes, you never saw so many cakes." Each woman measured her skill as a baker against her neighbors'. The old wood stoves had no thermostats; guesswork and experience were the only gauges. If you stuck your arm in the oven for a quick test and the hairs curled, you knew it was too hot.

Boats inevitably played a huge role in daily life. The youngsters rowed skiffs, and if there was a breeze, they cut down a short cedar tree and used it for a sail. Cedars in this marshy country grow wild, are prickly and dense enough to catch and hold a breeze. Shallow-rooted, they blow over in a high wind.

Baseball, a favorite sport on the Eastern Shore, developed some hot rivalries. When the Hoopers Island team was due to come up and challenge the James Island team, a reporter was reassured that "our boys will receive them kindly." Maps of the time show an uninterrupted road connecting the two points and overland travel along this bay shore route was still feasible at the end of the 19th Century.

Some betting on boats took place when the men gathered at the store. There seems to have been general agreement that the finest painted boat on James Island was Captain McNamara's. But who had the best bugeye? Whose canoe was the fastest? Was it Captain Phil Geohegan? Or Captain George Horner? A report from the period tells that "Capt. Horner generally manages to back down all opposed to him by producing a counterfeit hundred dollar bill."

Watermen had no trouble making a living. Catching fish in pound nets, crabbing, and tonging for oysters produced heavy catches. The problem was getting their produce to market. Asked by a starry-eyed outsider if he missed the days of sail, a local man replied: "I can tell you ain't never been beca'med[3] in the middle of the bay with a boatload of cantaloupes and crabs a-rottin' and a-stinkin."

By of the middle of the 18th century steamboats traveled regularly between Baltimore and ports on the shore, and a convenient landing would have given James Islanders ready access to more distant markets. As late as 1890, a letter to the editor of a Cambridge newspaper pleaded: "Now if the Maryland Steamboat Company will give us a wharf in Oyster Creek we will be one of the garden spots of Dorchester. Fish and crabs are in abundance, which, if there were any way of shipping them, would bring hundreds of dollars right at home."

He was whistling past the graveyard. Already his neighbor James C. Leonard, out oystering one day around 1885, realized

---

[3] Becalmed -- stuck in a rut, to landlubbers

his boat was floating over a spot he had once farmed as a youth. And he knew it was time to leave. Subsidence and erosion were taking their toll. His granddaughter, Barbara Zeigler, on a visit to Cambridge in 1988, told how he loaded his wife Mariah and their children, Mollie, Adelie, Edith and John, onto a barge and moved to Cambridge. James' brother Ivy, married to Mariah's sister Mollie, soon followed.

However, the 1890 census showed a score of families still hanging on, among them two Meekins families, two Maguire families along with Caleb McNamara and his painted boat, clinging to hope, refusing to face the inevitable.

Finally, erosion in the wake of storms brought the community to its knees. The causeway, known as the sand road, that had connected James to Taylor's Island was washed out in a storm not long after the turn of the century.

Captain Robert Shenton, born on Taylor's Island in 1900, could faintly remember as a small child, riding over the "sand road" up to James Island with his father in their buggy. And Bill Keene, Robert's contemporary, on a trip with his father, remembers seeing the pathetic sight of an abandoned bedstead in a ruined house, a trellis of roses out front, neglected but still blooming.

Meteorological records show that in 1903 and 1904 violent "Atlantic Coast Storms" roared up the east coast of the United States. Severe erosion inevitably followed in their wake and with the loss of its land link to Taylor's Island, and beyond, James Island was doomed.

People looked back and remembered the bird of evil omen -- a buzzard with a bell around its neck they had seen soaring over the island as the 20th century dawned. The superstitious said it was the Archangel Gabriel come to warn of the end of the world. Who would say they were wrong?

By the beginning of the 21st Century there were a few tattered clumps of land still to be seen where James Island had once flourished. Another vanished island.

Just south lay Taylor's Island.

Augustine Herrman self-portrait as shown on his map

Taylor's Island

Wingfield Point

A map of "Maryland and Virginia As it is Planted and Inhabited this present Year 1670 Surveyed and Exactly Drawne by the Only Labour and Endeavour of Augustin Herrman, Bohemiensis" labels as "Wingfield Pt" the area we now call Taylor's Island. Herrman has been called "the greatest personage of his day on the Eastern Shore." His thorough and detailed map shows plantations, a ship under full sail at the mouth of the "Potowmeck" River, "Indian Houses and Plantations," and a wealth of additional detail.

The map shows Poplar Island, "Sharpe's Ile," the Choptanck River, the Little Choptanck River and James Pt. It clearly labels Slaughter Creek. A town on the mainland to the east is called "Tobaco Stoks," later known as Tobacco Stick and today, Madison.

Augustin Herrman's map shows six dwellings on Wingfield Point, now known as Taylor's Island, and three on "James Point." We have seen that in 1662 Armstrong's Hogpen stood on the north shore of James Island. In the same year, the Taylor family -- Mr. and Mrs. Thomas Taylor and Tom's brother John Taylor -- crossed the Bay from St. Mary's County to claim a grant of 300 acres which they named Taylor's Folly. Naming one's newly acquired estate a folly carried no implication of foolishness or foolhardiness. Its true meaning in the 17th century, the O.E.D. says, was "delight" or "favorite abode."

The Taylors appear again, executing the earliest land deed in Dorchester County's Land Records, their sale of a 1,200-acre tract called "Taylor's Inheritance" to one Arthur Wright. That was in 1669. And then, having given their name to the erstwhile Wingfield Point, the Taylors disappear.

A feature of Herrman's map that merits a close look is the way he depicts the southern reaches of Wingfield Point, and may explain why he does not label the area an Island. He

9

shows Slaughter Creek petering out at its southernmost reaches before it meets the Bay. There is a thin ambiguous line at the bottom of Wingfield Point and a case might be made that it was attached at that time to the landmass of Dorchester County. It's a remarkable map by a remarkable man. Herrman was born in Prague in the Kingdom of Bohemia. The exact date is disputed, but 1605 comes close. His Protestant parents moved to Holland when he was a boy and as a young man he came to the New World in the employ of a Dutch trading company. He grew tobacco in Virginia and developed a profitable export business. And he owned a fleet of ships. The story of this enterprising, swashbuckling well-born gentleman who made his mark and his fortune in the 17th century has been highly romanticized in the telling.

He owned property in New Amsterdam, then governed by Peter Stuyvesant. It was easy to run athwart of Stuyvesant whose reputation as a hot-tempered man was widely known. Herrman is reputed to have once escaped prison in New Amsterdam by feigning insanity, riding his white horse on imaginary military maneuvers in the building where he was held, and at an opportune moment, in the wee hours of the morning, leaping through a window 15 feet above the ground, riding off, swimming across the Hudson River and eventually escaping to safe haven in New Castle, Delaware. The state of Delaware did not yet exist at that time. The area was still considered a part of Pennsylvania.

But there is little need to add spice to Herrman's actual adventures. Not only was he a successful entrepreneur and diplomat, he was a talented draftsman. In 1659 he began work on his map of Maryland and Virginia. In return for his labor he received a large tract of land in Cecil County, Maryland -- clearly marked on his map -- where he built Bohemia Manor and named the river that flowed nearby, the Bohemia. According to one biographer[4], "it took Herrman eight to ten years to gather the material for the map, at a total expenditure

---

[4] *Augustine Herrman, Beginner of the Virginia Tobacco Trade, Merchant of New Amsterdam and First Lord of Bohehmia Manor in Maryland.* Earl L. W. Heck, Englewood, Ohio, 1941.

of some two hundred pounds of money (equivalent to about five thousand dollars in [1941] currency)." The original map was drawn in four sections and sent to a London engraver named William Faithhorne to be completed, and in 1674 it was advertised for sale at shops in London. Only two copies of the original engraving are thought to exist, one in the British Museum and one in the John Carter Brown Library in Providence, R. I. Herrman's own work seems not to have survived. A copy was "compiled and edited by Edward H. Richardson Associates, Inc. consulting engineers of Newark, Delaware. Details photocopied and drafted from copies of originals owned by the Royal British Museum and by the John Carter Brown Library." It is from this reproduction that the Herrman self-portrait was copied.

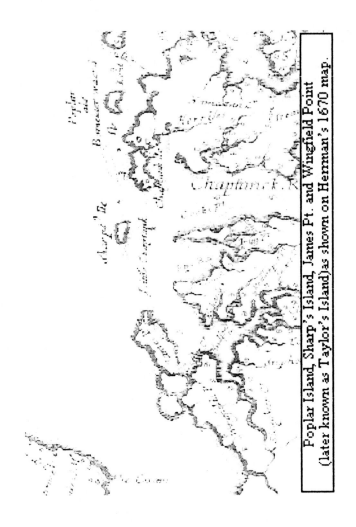

Poplar Island, Sharp's Island, James Pt. and Wingfield Point
(later known as Taylor's Island) as shown on Herrman's 1670 map.

"Water, Water, Everywhere"

Legend holds that Dorchester County has as much shoreline as the entire Eastern Seaboard of the United States put together. Unlikely? Take into account its every inlet, gut, bay and creek -- not to mention rivers with names like Choptank, Chicamacomico, Nanticoke and Transquaking --and you may become a believer. One source credits the county with 1,700 miles of shoreline, while pointing out that it's hard to tell where land ends and water begins. Almost 30 percent of the County is deemed wetlands.

Taylor's Island, a part of Dorchester County, claimed 1,100 acres in the year 2000. The Maryland Department of Natural Resources website reported: "The tidal marshes of Taylor's Island have been relatively untouched by the development of small towns and villages on the nearby shores. Small 'islands' of loblolly pine and cedar forest dot the marsh system. This large island . . . is a classic illustration of Chesapeake Bay tidal marsh habitat."

Roughly 12 miles long and at the widest point about 6 miles across, its marshy terrain is threaded with small creeks which divide the dry land into "necks."

In the never-ending battle between dry land and the waves that wash the shore, the water will always win. Put your money on it. Day after day, year after year, the Chesapeake Bay chews away at its banks with varying degrees of ferocity. High winds build waves that wash away farmland, bulkheads and even houses.

The epitome of futility is a bulkhead sitting forlornly out in the water, forty feet from the shoreline it was built at some expense to protect. It was not up to the job. No matter how soundly you may build a wall, how deeply you may set its foundation, soon you will notice that the waves have discovered its vulnerabilities. They come lapping in around either end, sweeping away the earth at the corners. Day by day, little by little, you can see their inroads. Then, a violent storm erupts. Mountainous waves spill over the top of the wall, snatch a great mouthful of good solid earth and take it away, only to come back for bite after bite.

A hurricane sweeps in with ferocious winds. Now the waves literally claw away at the land, declaring war on this too, too solid earth that literally melts. The bulkhead stands several feet out in the water, a futile, defeated structure. The narrow southern end of Taylor's Island takes a beating. This spit of land is bordered on the east by St. John's Creek. On the west, the Chesapeake Bay chomps away, taking hunks out of the blacktop on Punch Island Road which once led to an island that is no more.

In 1968-69 a battery of wrecked automobiles interlarded with discarded refrigerators was strewn along a stretch of Punch Island Road. It proved to be nothing more than the eyesore of the century. The Bay licked its chops and gobbled up this feast of rusted metal. Within a year or two there was not a vestige of this improvised bulkhead left.

The present technique of staving off erosion involves the use of rip-rap, a combination of a heavy black plastic sheet permeated with minute holes. Enormous boulders hold the plastic in place. The waves break over the boulders, and as the water seeps through the holes, the earth and sand are left behind. For some years, this system has effectively protected the Punch Island Road.

Taylor's Island's northern shore, once sheltered in the lee of James Island, now lies unprotected and in jeopardy.

Slaughter Creek, on Its eastern bank, separates the island from the mainland. This benign body of water provides a channel for work boats heading out to the Bay and day sailors who frequent the marina that lies on the mainland. It causes little or no erosion.

Looking through the keyhole
Of history at the 1700s

Introducing Henry Travers

In 1738, Henry Travers managed to scrape together 2,000 pounds of tobacco, 30 pounds in currency, and one pistole to buy 27 acres of land on Taylor's Island from Joseph Meekins. There is something pathetic about that one pistole. We will never know if Mr. Meekins was a skinflint, extracting every last pistole from a young man trying to get a start, or a generous landowner giving a young man a leg-up. It doesn't matter a great deal. The Travers family flourished on Taylor's Island and, thanks to one of its descendents who collected family documents and left them to posterity, we know a great deal about them.

The facts about the sale are set forth in an indenture, written in a fine legible copperplate hand at the time of the transaction. It's on file in the Maryland Room of the Cambridge.

The pistole was a gold coin of Spanish or Portuguese origin which circulated in the colonies and was often substituted for dwindling supplies of British currency. Sometimes a pistole was cut into several pieces. Henry's was apparently in tact. Although the colonists imported goods from abroad in quantity, and paid cash for them, their own economy was largely based on trade or barter, like Henry's 2,000 pounds of tobacco which he may have grown himself. A tobacco farmer near Upper Marlboro, Maryland, says a good rule of thumb in his day, before the bottom fell out of the tobacco market in the waning years of the 20th century, was 5,000 plants per acre. A stick -- the unit of tobacco that goes to market -- represents five or six plants, and weighs about six pounds. While we cannot know how skilled Henry was as a tobacco farmer, he could have grown the 2,000 pounds on a plot smaller than an acre.

The 27-acre property was called Robson's Folly and lay on the western side of the island -- on the Bay Shore. It is highly unlikely that any vestige of this land exists today, considering the insatiable appetite of Chesapeake Bay.

The indenture recording the bill of sale is worded in the archaic language of its day. It keeps the reader skipping across the centuries with phrases like: "...have given, granted, bargained, sold, aliened, ensconced and confirmed . . ." the deal. Legalese, with a flair.

The boundaries of this piece of land were laid out in a survey that started with a "bounded red oak." Concrete monuments were not yet in use. Trees, while commonly used to demarcate boundaries, could be felled or die, creating doubt and confusion, as the story of the Homny Pot will show later on. The exact location of the red oak is a bit vague, as well. It stands, the indenture says, "in or near" a parcel of land belonging to "one Taylors" and "above the head of a creek called St. Johns Creek."

The property line then runs southwest for 70 perches. A perch, equal to 5.5 yards was the universal unit of land measure at that time; 300 perches would approach a mile. Following on around we arrive at a "bounded gum tree" and finally come back to the red oak.

Indentures

Throw "indenture" into a word association game, and the answer, nine times out of ten, would come back "servant."

An indenture was simply a contract between two or more people and the term derived from the fact that one edge of the paper or parchment on which it was written, was notched or scalloped, or trimmed in such a way that all copies would line up, ensuring that they were genuine.

The practice has a long history. A gett, a Jewish divorce document, is torn at one corner. In *Henry IV*, part one, Shakespeare has Edmund Mortimer, Earl of March, say, as he divides the kingdom into three parts: "And our indentures tripartite are drawn, which being sealed interchangeably . . ."

Black's Law Dictionary says:

"indent, v.: To cut in a serrated or wavy line. In old conveyancing, if a deed was made by more parties than one, it

16

was usual to make as many copies of it as there were parties, and each was cut or indented (either in acute angles, like the teeth of a saw, or in a wavy line) at the top or side, to tally or correspond with the others, and the deed so made was called an 'indenture.' Anciently, both parts were written on the same piece of parchment, with some word or letters written between them through which the parchment was cut, but afterwards, the word or letters being omitted, indenting came into use, the idea of which was that the genuineness of each part might be proved by its fitting into the angles cut in the other."

As indentured servants flooded into the Colonies under contract to work seven years for a landholder, after which time they were free to go their way, both master and servant needed a verifiable copy of the agreement. Hence, "indentured servants."

Not all who signed up worked out their seven years. Some remained the scoundrels they were when they boarded ship in England to escape debt, prison or disgrace. Advertisements for runaway indentured servants, with descriptions like, "Has short beard, likes to gamble" appeared in local papers.

Others, however, having lived up to the terms of their indenture and worked out their time, received land as compensation, prospered and founded families that rose to prominence.

Women's Rights

In October 1738, three weeks after the date on the bill of sale for Robson's Folly, Henry Travers appeared before two of his Lordship's Justices of the Peace for Dorchester County to complete the formalities. He brought with him a friend named Benjamin Keene to serve as witness.

Joseph Meekins, the seller, brought along his wife, Elizabeth. At that time Elizabeth was "privately examined as the Law Directs [and] freely acknowledged" her agreement to the sale of the property.

"Being first privately examined" is the exact wording of the document.

And, with all the formalities out of the way, the deed was delivered to Henry to be recorded by Dorchester County Clerk H. Goldsborough on November 17, 1738. Since Henry had brought a friend, one assumes he was not yet married.

The procedure of protecting a woman's rights to jointly owned property continued in practice. When Pollard North sold a tract called Robson's Lott, in December 1804, Mrs. North was similarly consulted in private.

The deed states that Mrs. North, who was known as Polly, "privately and out of the hearing of her husband was asked whether she doth make her acknowledgment of the same willingly and freely, and without being induced thereto by fear or threats of, or ill usage by, her husband, or fear of his displeasure."

In 1786, 48 years after Henry bought his 27 acres, an Elizabeth Travers, identified by one source as the widow of Henry Travers, was given permission to operate her late husband's ferry across Slaughter Creek. Elizabeth got a fee of 37 pounds, 10 shillings annually, provided she kept a ferryboat in good order that would safely carry six passengers and three horses across the stream at once. Members of the local population crossed free. "Strangers," however, paid six pence, with an additional shilling for each horse.

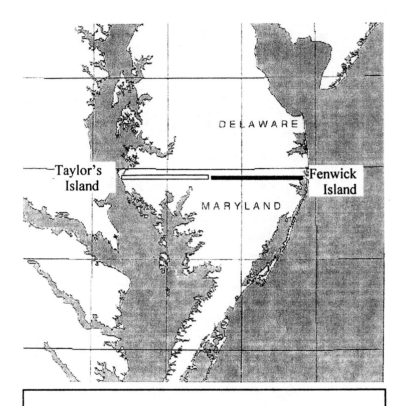

Taylor's Island

DELAWARE

Fenwick Island

MARYLAND

The line surveyed between the Atlantic Ocean and the Chesapeake Bay stretched from Fenwick Island to Taylor's Island. The center point of this line was central to the survey and was used to establish the southern boundary of Delaware as well as the point at which its western boundary extended northward.

Once the center point was set, the "ghost" line westward to Taylor's Island (shown in white) no longer had any significance and fell into history's trash.

The Mason-Dixon Line

The role Taylor's Island played in the surveying of the Mason-Dixon Line is rarely documented and difficult to research. Indeed, it's hard to find "Mason-Dixon Line" listed in the indices of books on Maryland's history. Fortunately, an historical marker in front of Grace Episcopal Church on Taylor's Island keeps the memory alive. The marker was put in place in 1959 with considerable fanfare. Governor Millard Tawes and U.S. Senator George L. Radcliffe, both born on the Eastern Shore, as well as the Bishop of the Diocese of Easton, were present at its unveiling.

It reads:

CHAPEL OF EASE
OLD TRINITY EPISCOPAL CHURCH

In the selection of the middle point between the Atlantic Ocean and the Chesapeake Bay for the start of the Mason Dixon line survey, this area was the center of a long controversy among British, Md. and Pa. officials as to whether Taylors Island was part of the main land or an Island. An adverse decision resulted in the loss of land to Pa. now Delaware.

Md. Historical Society

These little markers cram so much information into so little space that confusion is bound to result. Let's skip for the moment the reference to "Chapel of Ease and Old Trinity Episcopal Church" and focus on clarifying the text.

Old World monarchs sliced up lands in the New World and dealt out enormous tracts without benefit of surveys or any clear definition of boundaries. The territories were a long way from home and hostile Indians often served as deterrents to surveyors, as well. Disagreement inevitably arose over where one grant ended and another began. Such a boundary dispute raged between the Penns and the Calverts for years.

The Penns needed to establish where Pennsylvania began --
or ended --- if you were a Calvert. The Calverts needed to
know the northern limits of Maryland. Hostilities were
averted when the two parties finally agreed in April 1763 that
the Messrs Charles Mason and Jeremiah Dixon, astronomers,
should come over from England to survey the area and set a
border. Mason and Dixon arrived in Philadelphia in November
of that year.

The agreement stipulated that a line be drawn between the
Atlantic Ocean and the Chesapeake Bay. It would start at
Fenwick Island on the ocean and head west to Taylor's Island
on the   Bay. At its midpoint, a   line would be drawn
perpendicular to the base, extending north, and forming the
western boundary of Delaware. Delaware's southern boundary
would be formed by that part of the line between the Ocean and
the midpoint. The resulting tidy little state with a right-angled
boundary appears on maps today.

However, since that part of the line west of the mid-point and
extending to the Bay would have no practical use, it would
simply be ignored as if it had never existed. It would be erased,
as if it had never been drawn. Not so strange, after all, that the
role of Taylor's Island in this drama has been forgotten.

The survey of the western extension of the line, however,
developed a hitch.   The question arose of whether Taylor's
Island was truly an island or just a promontory. On Herrman's
map, we have seen, it was labeled Wingfield Point.   And
Herrman was considered a fine cartographer.

Senator George Radcliffe, at whose behest the historical
marker had been placed, writes: "The Penn family raised the
preposterous point that Taylor's Island should not be
considered an island but included in the mainland when seeking
to ascertain the middle point of [the line between the Atlantic
Ocean and the Chesapeake Bay].

"The controversy was carried to Great Britain," Radcliffe
continues. "The astonishing thing is that the contention of Penn
prevailed.   Therefore the boundary between Maryland and
Delaware is now nearly two miles further west than it would
have been if the sound contention of Lord Baltimore [that
Taylor's Island WAS an island] had prevailed.   And Delaware

has approximately 150 square miles that would otherwise be a part of the Eastern Shore of Maryland." This, in spite of the fact that "in 1751 a large map was carefully prepared of Taylor's Island, after a survey, by commissioners representing Lord Baltimore and William Penn. This map shows, of course, that Taylor's Island was and is an island separated by broad waters from the mainland. The original of this large map, over 200 years old, is in the possession of the Maryland Historical Society." Vestiges of Mason's and Dixon's monumental survey are hard to find today. In1766 the surveyors began setting markers. The one-mile stones bore the initials of the two contesting areas and were placed so that the P faced Pennsylvania and the M faced Maryland. The five-mile markers were handsomely carved with the coats of arms of the Penn and Calvert families. Only a few of these stones have survived to this day. Two or three of them have been preserved in a shelter along Route 54 between Delmar, Delaware and Mardela, Maryland.

The "double-shouldered" chimney at the rear of the Chapel of Ease. The head- stones are in the Grace Church graveyard.

Chapel of Ease
Old Trinity Episcopal Church

Let's get back to the first two lines of that historical marker.
What, exactly, *is* a Chapel of Ease?
It's defined as a church built within the bounds of a parish for the attendance of those who cannot reach the parish church conveniently.
Old Trinity Church, established around 1685, is located in Church Creek, a village on the mainland about 15 miles east of Taylor's Island. Going to church there would have involved taking the family across Slaughter Creek on a ferry and traveling down a road we might not dignify with that description today.
It was far easier for a clergyman on horseback to make it over the creek and through the woods to a Chapel of Ease where he could administer the sacraments, performing rites like weddings and baptisms, and do some preaching as well. Once arrived, he could expect to enjoy the hospitality of a prominent family and join in a covered dish supper for which the area became widely famous.
The Chapel was built around 1710 (there is no certainty about the date) on the banks of Slaughter Creek, presumably convenient to the ferry landing. It is a sizeable building, some 32 by 21 feet in dimension. At one end there is a small gallery with steps leading up to it. And there is debate about its original purpose -- slave gallery or choir loft? Again, no one knows for sure.
An architect named Finlay Ferguson who, in 1956 was involved with the restoration of Old Trinity Church, visited the Chapel and wrote this to Senator Radcliffe:
". . .the little chapel on Taylor's Island . . . is extremely interesting and it is very unusual to find a frame building with exposed girders and corner posts today. I described it to several in Williamsburg and they were much interested. It certainly is worth every effort to restore it. The gallery is, as far as I know, unique and a most interesting survival. It is

25

similar as I remember it to the wooden Meeting House in Easton which . . . is also 17th Century."

The building was used not only for religious purposes but also, according to Senator Radcliffe to whom Taylor's Island history was an avocation, as a meeting place for civic and governmental functions. He adds an interesting note: "Since the church was controlled by Lord Baltimore, he appointed the rectors and every man was required by law to contribute forty acres of tobacco each year for the up-keep of the church." That's a whale of a lot of tobacco.

After Grace Church opened its doors in 1873 the Chapel of Ease lost its *raison d'etre* and was sold. But not forgotten. In 1952, some 250 years after it was built, the old building was moved at a cost of $400 to the grounds surrounding Grace Church. When its restoration was completed in 1959, Senator Radcliffe urged the community to make use of it for meetings or other events -- perhaps even as a museum. And the members of the Taylor's Island Homemakers Club took him up on the offer, holding June covered dish luncheons there.

"Chapel of Ease -- Old Trinity Episcopal Church" earned its mentioned on the historical marker that stands beside its present location.

Shipwash's Homney Pot

On December 25, 1782, the Justices of Dorchester County Court swore in Thomas Lockerman and John King to take depositions about a boundary dispute. Wait -- December 25 is Christmas day! But in 1782, December 25 was a day like any other. Christmas had not yet been designated a legal holiday; it was then exclusively a religious observance.

The disputed boundary was on "a tract of land called Taylors Folly. . . the bounds whereof are decayed and likely to be lost." Taylor's Folly is that 300-acre plot the Taylors took over in 1662. You may be sure the boundaries were marked by trees, the universal boundary markers of the era.

The 1670 Herrman map of Virginia and Maryland pictures a double line of trees marking the Eastern Shore boundary between the two states. Herrman notes: "These Limits between VIRGINIA and MARYLAND are thus bounded by both sides' Deputies the 27 May 1668 marked by dubble Trees from this Pokomake EAST to the seaside to a creeke called Swansecut."

Back to Taylor's Folly. Now it's 1782, more than one hundred years have gone by, and "one Henry Traverse" has petitioned the Justices to have "a Commission to examine evidences to prove and perpetuate the memory of the bounds..."

To settle this dispute the Messrs. Lockerman and King were required to sit out of doors in the January cold beside a dead pine tree and take down in writing eight long-winded depositions. These documents lack any punctuation. All are written in the form of a single long run-on sentence, never pausing for breath, period, comma or semicolon. The format is apparently intended to preclude alteration of the wording after the fact, much as indentures assured the authenticity of a copy of a document.

The deponents were as variegated a bunch of men as you are likely to put together. They ranged from educated younger men to semi-literate old coots. And while their testimony is often long-winded and dull, it nevertheless opens a window on colloquial language and usage.

The pithiest was the first: "Thomas Woollen, aged 54 years or thereabouts being sworne on the Holy Evangels of Almighty God in relation to the third bounder of a tract of land called Taylors Folly deposeth and sayeth that at the place where this Deposition was taken he saw a pine lying down and his Father told him not to cut it for it was a bounder of Traverses land. And further saith not." Time to take a breath!

A long-winded gent named John Pagan, about 70 years old, tells how he had heard that a certain Robson "was with them when they run Taylors Folly from the Bay they run the number of perches and said here ought to be a bounder keep on and look out and they kept along and Robson says Where are you going? If you go any further you'll be in Shipwashes Homney Pot and they stopped and marked a pine."

Now heed Richard Patterson, also some 70 years old, who remembered running a course 320 perches from the bay, at which point "they stopped and looked about for a bounded tree and found none he said John Robson if we go much farther on this course we shall be in Phillip Williams Homney Pot then they all stopped and looked about for a bounder but found none."

The message is clear. "Shipwash" was not a man to be trifled with. He did not take kindly to trespassers. An unspoken "Whoa" accompanies the sound of his name.

There are two lessons here:

1. Steer clear of Phillip "Shipwash" Williams. Do not trespass on his Homny Pot.

2. Use stone markers, like Mason and Dixon did.

# # #

For the information of genealogists who may be combing these pages, the following information also came to hand:

Some months after the first depositions, additional statements were taken from a number of Travers family members.

Henry Travers who bought Robson's Folly in 1738 may be the grandfather Henry Travers, Jnr, mentions in his deposition. He says "his grandfather Traverse told him about fifteen years ago or more that at the place where the aforesaid depositions was taken the bounder of Taylors Folly stood . . ."

28

And there John Travers, "Senr aged about 71 years," said that "about 40 years ago Col'n Henry Travers and his brother William told him that the dead Pine now standing where this deposition was taken was the third bounder of the land called Taylors Folly..."

And here comes yet another Travers -- William Henry -- who ran the ferry across Slaughter Creek that Elizabeth took over in 1786. One John Budd Senior recalled that "about thirty-one or thirty-two years ago walking up this road that leads from Wm. Henry Traverses Ferry that Col'n Henry Traverse deceased pointed to a pine tree and say'd there stand a bounder of Taylors Folly ... and say'd it was the third bounder...".

On October 15th of 1783, the two deposers had finished their job and "certified that we the Commissioners have met on the said land and have taken the above depositions agreeable to the Commission. Witness our hands this 15th day of October 1783. Thos. Lockerman, John King."

The Becky Phipps and her Shrine

The Becky Phipps

The instant you arrive on Taylor's Island history greets you in the form of a little cannon, a relic of the War of 1812, with a marker placed by the DAR. It reads:

> The Becky Phipps.
>
> This cannon was taken from a British tender in 1814. Lieut. Phipps and Crew of 17 men and one colored woman were taken prisoners at James Point by Capt. Joseph Stewart's Company of Militia composed of men from Taylor's Island and Tobacco Stick.

Robert G. Stewart, a descendant of Capt. Joseph, did a thorough job of researching his ancestor's experience. He has called the marker "inaccurate in the extreme." And he is well-qualified to point out its inaccuracies.

But you might as well tell the Swiss that William Tell was a lousy marksman as to cast doubt about the Becky Phipps on Taylor's Island. Who, after all, knows better than the DAR? There *was* a Becky, as the marker says. So what if Lieut. Phipps actually spelled his name Phibbs? The name of the cannon is, make no mistake about it, The Becky Phipps.

By 1814, Robert Stewart explains in a monograph (see note at end of chapter), the British Navy had blockaded the Chesapeake Bay and raiding parties regularly came ashore scouting American farms for provender. They helped themselves to sheep, cattle, poultry and any other groceries they could find. Fed up with these depredations, the local people -- landowners, farmers, and shipbuilders --formed militias. Joseph Stewart, the owner of a plantation near Cambridge, joined up, along with men named Travers, Spicer, Cator, Navy, Keene, Edmondson, Tall, Geohegan and LeCompte.

The *Dauntless*, one of the British ships of war plying the waters of the Bay, had been a singularly successful marauder. She had burned a couple of American vessels and captured a

31

sloop bearing 14 casks of whiskey and another ship with a cargo of 200 gallons of beer.

Lieut. Phibbs had come aboard the *Dauntless* after serving in the Mediterranean and the East Indies. During that bitter winter of 1814 he must have suffered acutely from the cold; nevertheless on February 5th he succeeded in stealing seven sheep from the Geohegan farm on James Island and had made the mistake of threatening to come back for more. That alerted the militia.

On February 6, 1815, the *Dauntless* was anchored off James Island when her master spotted three American schooners heading down the Little Choptank River toward the Bay. He sent the shivering Phibbs out with a longboat and a jolly boat to see what damage he could do. These smaller craft served the warship as a means of negotiating shallow waters and reaching shore.

The following morning the *Dauntless*, herself, was icebound. Historian Stewart says that "By evening the Master noted in his log 'fresh breezes with severe frost the boats not having returned fear they are frozen in.'" He was dead right. And the weather was perfect for the formation of an ice mound.[5] By the next day Phibbs' boat was also stuck firmly between an ice mound on the shore and a big cake of ice that had drifted in from the Bay. A sitting duck.

The militiamen on Taylor's Island were quick to realize their advantage. The ice mound would be a great place from which to launch an attack. But getting over to it proved dicey since the ice cover had broken up and there were many dangerously thin spots to be skirted. Following Joseph

---

5 Ice mounds, while not commonplace, do form in the Bay after a hard freeze. Ice chunks, broken up by the tidal flow, pile up into great ersatz icebergs. In February 1918 a 40-foot-high pile of ice chunks formed on the shore of Taylor's Island. It was something to see. Mrs. Daniel B. Prettyman who lived on the Island with her Methodist minister husband, writing about the phenomenon later, said: "We wrapped ourselves up snugly, got into our Page [an automobile of that era] and drove over to see it." She recalled the incident in an article printed in the Baltimore Sun of December 11, 1960 accompanied by a picture of the mound.

Stewart's lead, a group made it safely across, took up positions on the ice mound and starting firing at the tender.

Capt. Joseph Stewart's original account says the engagement lasted a couple of hours until one of the men on board the ship was shot in the neck, whereupon the entire crew came on deck, waved white handkerchiefs and "cryed out for Quarter."

In addition to Phibbs and his men, a black woman named Becky and a black man, Abraham Travers, also surrendered.

Taken from the ship was a cannon, a "12-pound carronade" which over the years was christened the Becky Phipps. It became the custom on Taylor's Island to fire her to celebrate the Fourth of July and other patriotic occasions.

Across the years she boomed away without a hitch. Then, an excess of zeal proved her undoing. An overly enthusiastic young Islander, Joe Lambden, celebrating the victory of Woodrow Wilson over two candidates -- Teddy Roosevelt and William Howard Taft -- served her up a double load. The Becky Phipps blew sky high, raining pieces down on roads and rooftops. And, legend has it, the uproar so startled Bill Keene's mother, that she forthwith gave birth to the infant William.

What is left of the Becky Phipps is now sheltered in a small shrine on the right after you have crossed the new bridge to Taylor's Island.

Note___

When he was curator of the National Portrait Gallery in Washington, Robert G. Stewart, descended from Capt. Joseph Stewart, who led the Battle of the Ice Mound, researched this event. He had access to Archives in the Nation's Capital and produced a scholarly paper titled "The Battle of the Ice Mound, February 7, 1815." The *Maryland Historical Magazine* published it in Vol. 70, No. 4. Winter 1975. This paper is the source for this account.

Grace Protestant Episcopal Church

The 19th Century

I've Got a Beautiful Feeling . . .

Prosperity kissed Taylor's Island during the years that followed the War of 1812 bringing tangible rewards as well as small refinements. The Methodists organized a Temperance Union in 1832, and soon afterward, the men of the island met at a "Lyceum," a cultural group that flourished for a good many years. Shipping thrived. A three-masted barque built in the area carried on commerce with South American countries under the command of a master from Taylor's Island. In 1854 a bridge spanned Slaughter Creek. Fourteen years later -- years interrupted by the Civil War -- a wharf was built and connected to the bridge. The Episcopalians opened a large new church and bade the Chapel of Ease farewell.

Benjamin Harrington opened a tomato cannery where he packed Pride brand tomatoes. And the Emma Giles came steaming down Slaughter Creek to tie up at the new wharf, bringing the greatest excitement of all.

The century treated Taylor's Island very well.

Temperance

Liquor was never in short supply on the Eastern Shore. Around 1800 there were over 600 distilleries there, most of them in Dorchester County. To be fair, Dorchester *is the* largest county in the state of Maryland. Fifty years earlier one Roger Addams of Dorchester, when drunk, bet that he could "Drink all of the Wine there was left in a Decanter at one Draught. He won the Wager, but Died a few Minutes after." (*Maryland Gazette* of May 5. 1761.) [6]

---

[6] *The Americans. A Social History of the United States 1587 - 1914.* Furnas. This book has given me many insights in to life in colonial times.

Tradition was on the drinkers' side. Alcohol played a sizable role in colonial times when everybody drank -- men, women and teenagers. Beer or wine with meals was expected, starting with breakfast.

Whiskey, Holland gin, apple brandy, New England rum, French brandy, Jamaica spirits, Madera, Sherry, Port and Lisbon wines were available in an Easton shoppe starting as early as 1805.

Field hands in the mid-nineteenth century demanded liquor at harvest time -- they believed it was unsafe to drink the water without purifying it with a tot of alcohol, and who is to say they were wrong? Newspapers carried advertisements for "Harvest Liquors" --common whisky, brandy, gin and rum. Ordinary whiskey cost 18 cents a gallon if you bought it by the barrel. If you just wanted a gallon or two you brought your own jug and paid a few cents more.

The cause of Temperance was waiting in the wings. In 1830 a young man named Levi Travers took pen in hand and wrote an essay which began: "If there ever was an evil under the broad canopy of Heaven it is drinking of ardent spirits." He supported this thesis with endless arguments in rotund prose and he sounds like an earnest young person. He must have convinced folks, because a couple of years later, on January 23, 1832, the Taylor's Island Temperance Society was founded.

Its Constitution stipulated that the Society would attack the evils of drink with "no other weapon but argument, persuasion and the influence of good example." Ninety-seven signatures were appended in two columns--men's on the left, women's on the right.

Moderation was the theme of the Temperance movement. Not abstinence. Moderation. A Board of Managers was empowered "if it is deemed advisable, [to] circulate tracts or other writing calculated to invite the attention of the publick to the horrors of intemperance, its cause and remedies."

But down here in Article 7, we find this curious locution:

"Whereas the use of wines and cordials leads to intemperance we therefore whose names are herein attested do pledge ourselves to drink no wines or cordials except in extreme cases of necessity as a medicine and on sacramental occasions." Now this sounds a lot more like abstinence than temperance.

One signer, Henry G. Navy, appears to have fallen off the wagon so hard that his name was stricken from the list of signers, many of whom were members of the old families on both James and Taylor's Islands. The president's name was Travers. William Geoghegan was vice president and an Edmondson -- a family that lived in Cator cove -- was secretary. Other names were Levi D. Travers, Sr., father of young Levi who wrote the passionate essay condemning the drinking of "ardent spirits," and Thomas Keene of L., a curious abbreviation. It appears again in the records of the Lyceum of which he was a founding member.

BETHLEHEM METHODIST
EPISCOPAL CHURCH
BUILT 1787 · REBUILT 1857
THE ORIGINAL CHAPEL WAS BUILT ON
THIS SITE WHICH WAS DONATED BY MOSES
AND ELIZABETH LE COMPTE. THE DEED, DATED
SEPTEMBER 15, 1787, IS THE OLDEST ONE ON
RECORD FOR METHODIST EPISCOPAL CHURCH
LAND IN DORCHESTER COUNTY.
BOTH BISHOP FRANCIS ASBURY AND REVEREND
FREEBORN GARRETTSON PREACHED HERE.

MARYLAND HISTORICAL SOCIETY

38

The Lyceum

Lyceum is not a word you hear any more, but in the 19th century it was commonly used for a literary institution or a lecture hall.   However unlikely it may seem, a lyceum was formed on Taylor's Island on January 5, 1842, when a group of men got together to form a "debating society which would serve as a lyceum for mutual instruction."

In populous areas, lyceums invited guest speakers to entertain and enlighten the audiences and they might meet once a month or as often as weekly.   The Taylor's Island Lyceum had a different timetable. The minutes show that it met only in January and February. The men were for the most part farmers who could take time off only when the earth was frozen and they were free to spend a little time away from their fields.

They met at the "Old School House," and a note penciled in later explains that it stood   "on Lu Brannock's lot at crossroads."   On that chilly January day, the   most urgent order of business was to delegate to the Tall brothers the job of procuring a stove, setting it up   and providing coal. That first meeting must have moved along at a good clip.

A Constitution was drawn up which set dues but the exact amount is hard to decipher.   A subsequent revision of the rules required an initiation fee of ten cents with monthly dues of five cents.

Speakers were limited to 15 minutes per presentation, and two or three men were expected to come   prepared to give a recitation.

The minutes do not show at what hour the group met -- likely in the afternoon.   Traveling over rough icy roads at night and reading their papers by lamplight seems unlikely.   It's a safe guess that after the mid-day meal they forsook the "Farmers Journal" for a couple of hours to think on more frivolous matters.

They entered their rusty words in a ledger, the first 15 or 20 pages of which had been removed -- cut out cleanly out with a straight razor. The remaining pages, in mint condition, served the many secretaries over the years. Frugality was both a habit and a virtue.

The first debate of the new Lyceum addressed the subject: "Which affords the greatest degree of pleasure -- pursuit or possession?" The affirmative, the minutes tell us, won. Which was the affirmative?

Not all the debates considered serious topics. The men came to enjoy themselves.

"Which is more eligible for a wife, a widow or an old maid" was debated and the winner was old maid. There was latitude for levity and one debater spiced up his remarks with stories of sailors' cavorting with mermaids.

"Which is more admired -- personal or mental charms?" Personal, of course.

"Which is the greater evil -- ardent spirits or Pride?" This debate resulted in a tie, broken by the president's ruling in favor of "spiritous liquor."

Over the years the name of the group changed, called for a while the Polemical Society and later on, the Debating Society.

The last entry in the ledger is an essay by one of the leaders, Levi Travers, who we may presume to be the same Levi Travers who wrote so eloquently about the evils of strong drink in 1830. In February 20, 1853, now a mature man, he wrote on *The Beautiful.* He was a literate man and a born communicator.

The ledger served the Lyceum for ten years before it ran out of pages; the group may have continued it meetings, for all we know. One day another ledger, picking up where the original one left off, may come to light in an attic. The men who wrote up the minutes were conscientious, literate and their handwrirting was easily legible. Members included Traverses, Geoghegans, Talls, Edmondsons, Navys and Cators -- names that go back for generations. Toward the back of the book an anonymous secretary wrote in a beautiful hand the words:

"Evil communication corrupts good manners. Ovid"

It's a little work of art. An idle doodle? Or a comment on a member's offensive outburst?

Captain William Cator
of the Bark *Rainbow*

By the beginning of the 19th century tobacco had given way to wheat as the shore's principal crop. Up and down the Atlantic seaboard farmers found that Peruvian guano, the lime from seabirds that had accumulated for centuries on islands lying off Peru, gave their tired soil just the jolt it needed. Crops thrived and farmers relied on the timely arrival of this fertilizer at planting time. One year the economy was dealt a severe blow when cargoes of guano were late in arriving. As a consequence the wheat crop was poor and there was talk of taking the matter to Washington.

The sailing vessels that crowded the wharves and the waters of the Eastern Shore kept business and industry rolling along as surely as the 18-wheelers that roar across our roads from the Atlantic coast to the shores of the Pacific today. Farmers shipped out their wheat to foreign markets aboard barks and schooners and the vessels returned with cargoes of coffee, sugar and molasses, not to mention such exotic things as chocolate, allspice, ginger and tamarinds.

Captain William Cator, of Taylor's Island, commanded the *Rainbow*, a 757-ton three-masted merchant vessels called a bark built in 1845. She made several trips to Whampoa, a southern Chinese port (Huangpu today).

On one of her voyages the *Rainbow* came upon the *Billow*, a ship in distress off the coast of Brazil. Under Captain W. W. McGee she was headed for California with a group of Forty-Niners eager to strike it rich in the newly found gold fields. Captain Cator came to her rescue, enabling the *Billow* to continue her voyage around the The Horn and on up to the west coast.

Time passed. The *Rainbow* returned to homeport. And one day a package arrived for Captain Cator from Captain McGee. In it was a golden ring, finely worked, bearing a raised shield and anchor. Inscribed within were the names of the two captains and their ships.

A fitting thank you, which became a family heirloom.

William Cator left the ring to his son, Thomas, who in the early 1900s   ran a hotel and livery stable in Cambridge. Tom liked to wear the ring, but its soft gold had worn thin over the years, it was loose on his finger, and from time to time it slipped off while he was shoveling horse manure in his livery stable.   Nearby neighbors who tended vegetable gardens were steady customers for the manure.

Then the worst happened. The ring was gone, missing for days, weeks.   Tom was deeply fearful that it had gone down with a cargo of manure he had sold for shipment across the Bay to the Western Shore. He mourned his loss.   Nevertheless, he passed the word around among friends and neighbors to be on the lookout for it -- just in case.

The summer was drawing to an end when, one day, a neighbor's child arrived at the hotel with a large gift-wrapped box for Mr. Thomas Cator.   The youngster watched as Tom first unwrapped the large box, then the smaller box within it, and still another inside that one, and finally, a small box containing the Cator ring.   Tom's neighbor, pulling up beets for supper, noticed something embedded in one of them.   On looking more closely, he and his wife realized it was the famous Cator ring.   Knowing how Tom had mourned the loss of the family heirloom, the neighbors devised an ingenious way to get it back on his finger.

The Will

William Travers died in April 1857. His will paints an unflattering picture of the man who -- "being in perfect health of body and of sound and disposing mind memory and understanding, and considering the certainty of death and the uncertainty of the time thereof" -- wrote it.

The first order of business has to do with his daughter Eliza Jane who was not in good odor with her father. The wife's customary "thirds" of the estate taken care of, her father leaves her the balance -- with one proviso: that she "not mary (sic) Washington A. Smith, and if she doth mary said Washington A. Smith I give said Eliza Jane Travers one dollar and no more of my estate...".

Who was this Washington A. Smith and what was wrong with him? He was obviously an outsider. His name does not appear on the temperance pledge; he was not involved in the Lyceum; he was not a property owner. A foreigner! What other strikes he had against him we will never know, but to Mr. Travers, Washington A. Smith was anathema.

The inventory of the Travers house, recorded and attached to the will, lists absolutely everything, everything except possibly the dirt on the kitchen floor. All the pieces of furniture, the bedsteads, the feather beds and every piece of bed linen and every chamber pot are listed. The stove, even the lifter for the stove lids, every ladle and every pan. Even the "iron pot of grease on top of the stove" is listed.

Turn the page. To someone living in the 21st Century, it's a shocker.

Page 3 is a list of William Travers' slaves with their monetary value.

Here are their names: the men were: Steven, 60; Richard, 58; William, 52; Levi, 48; Cesar, 40; Levin, 45; John, 20; William John, 16; Jesse, 12; Sam, 4 and George, 1.

The women were: Rose, 36; Polly, 52; Mary P. and child, 20; Beate, 7; Leah, 4; Sarah 2; and Hester 26.

Their total value was $5,800.

Emancipation came to Maryland on November 1, 1864. It would be seven more years before these men, women and children would know freedom from slavery.

Along the roads leading to Taylor's Island are historical markers telling of Harriet Tubman and her Underground Railroad. She was born in Dorchester County not far from an area known as Golden Hill.

In the first half of the 19th century slavery existed on the Eastern Shore side by side with a movement known as the American Colonization Society, a group of people interested in returning slaves to Liberia. A ship called the *Mary Caroline Stevens*, financed by a businessman from Trappe and Easton, sailed for Liberia in December 1856 with freed slaves from both Maryland and Virginia. "Marylanders sought by sane and peaceful means, an answer to what they had long recognized as a problem that must be resolved." [7]

---

[7] 150 Years of Banking on the Eastern Shore, Elliott Buse. p. 99

Grace Church – Part One

The Civil War notwithstanding, the mid 1800s were yeasty years. In 1854 the first bridge was built across Slaughter Creek and some years later, in1869, a wharf was built and attached to it. Grace Protestant Episcopal Church, dedicated in May 1873, offers the best evidence of the optimism and faith in a prosperous future that dominated thinking on Taylor's Island. The church is spacious. Its beautiful walnut pews, a gift from a Baltimore lumber company, can accommodate 150 to 200 congregants. Its steeple, covered with cedar shakes, is capped with a cross. Its siding is white clapboard. It cost $3,500.

Three men, whose names go back to the Island's very beginnings, sparked its construction. Samuel M. Travers, whose wife, Eugenia, is credited with naming the Church, took charge of fund raising. Thomas Broome Travers gave the lot, boarded the carpenters and oversaw the job. J. L. Pattison, a generous contributor, was an invalid who died in September, a few months after the dedication. His was the first grave in the churchyard.

How did this triumvirate envision Taylor's Island's future? Did they believe they were standing on the brink of skyrocketing, post-war prosperity with a growing population? Were they anticipating a rosy future in shipbuilding on the Island, unprepared for the dominance of the steamboat? Were their hopes pinned on the surging cannery business? Or was there, perhaps, a competitive element present?

Just fifteen years earlier, in 1857, the Methodists had built a handsome church of "red brick, 45 feet long, 30 feet wide, green metal steeple, green shutters on 12 over 12 windows," according to one Duncan L. Noble, who wrote a brief history of the church. It stood across the road from the site of the old Bethlehem Meeting House, which was located on land given by Col. Moses LeCompte and his wife Elizabeth on Sept. 15, 1787 and that building remained in use until the new brick church was completed. Duncan Noble records that "Bethlehem was the first church in this section to divide from the M. E. Church because of the Controversy [over the issue of slavery] which divided Methodism."

Two handsome churches. Two active congregations. But the best laid plans . . .   We shall see.

Canneries

Tomato canning was perfected in 1847 at a small engineering school for young gentlemen named Lafayette College in Easton, Pennsylvania. And canneries took off. In the decades before 1900 they had sprung up far and wide on the Eastern Shore of Maryland and their numbers continued to increase, accounting for "an astonishingly large share of the nation's annual pack." *8   A compulsive counter of canneries named Moses Moore figured there were 187 in the general area of Cambridge where he lived. And, he believed, the first one to be built there in 1875 is the one that wound up in the hands of Albanus and Levi Phillips and grew into the nationally known Phillips Packing Company. Much of its fame rested on the unique flavor of the tomatoes that grow in the soil of Dorchester County.

Benjamin Harrington built a cannery on Taylor's Island right beside the   new wharf attached to the bridge.   Exactly when the establishment opened and when it closed is difficult to pin down.   A clue may lie in the fact that the steamboat Emma *Giles* began her regular passenger and freight service between Baltimore and the Island in 1887.

We know from his son Byron that Benjamin Harrington did a little dentistry on the side.   Byron, who in time took over the cannery, treasured a pair of forceps his father had used to pull teeth.   When he eventually turned them over to the Taylor's Island Museum, Byron attached a note explaining that when he was only nine years old, he had witnessed his father pulling a tooth for a neighbor, Travers Theophilis Spicer.   The sight, he said, "scared him half to death."

The Harringtons and their cannery lived fondly in the memory of men who had worked there as boys, earning the first cash money they ever carried in their pockets.

Almost a century later, a desk that survived the demise of the cannery yielded up an unexpected souvenir.   Cleaning out the old building that had once housed its offices to enlarge a country store, the new owner came across a supply of colored post cards advertising Pride brand tomatoes -- a souvenir of another day and age.

The Harringtons were a talented family. Byron's brother, Emerson, born in nearby Madison in 1865, would become governor of the state of Maryland from 1916 to 1920 and live to the age of 81. Honor came to him in1935 when the new bridge over the Choptank River at Cambridge was given his name.

This postcard in full color, advertised tomatoes
"Packed exclusively by
B. E. Harrington & Son
Taylor's Island
Maryland"

Emma Giles
The Dreamboat Steamboat

Although steamships began to offer passenger service on the Chesapake Bay early in the 19th century, it was not until 1887 that the Emma Giles sidled up to the wharf on Taylor's Island to take on passengers and freight for Baltimore. For almost fifty years, wind and tide permitting, the *Emma Giles* plied the waters of the Chesapeake Bay, her smokestacks, paddlewheel and round pilot house agleam in the sunlight. She carried 1,500 passengers and made two runs a week between Baltimore and Taylor's Island. She took tomatoes and cantaloupes from Dorchester farmers and brought back the little luxuries their wives depended on -- ten yards of lace, a piece of dress goods or a new pattern. At the sound of her name eyes lit up. She was the sweetheart of the Eastern Shore in the hearts of all who ever trod her decks

She was not just transportation. She opened the door to the wide, wide world. She offered the chance to say "yes" when opportunity knocked. She was a ticket out of the irksome ties of home; and the way back to the bosom of a loving family.

She fabricated memories. She fostered romance. Plying her course back and forth between Baltimore and the Eastern Shore, she wove an enduring thread into the fabric of her passengers' lives. Take Bill Keene. His parents -- William Eugene and Kate Allen -- met aboard her. Five years later Kate abandoned her career as a dressmaker in Greenwich Village, New York, to marry the young man trying to turn a profit in his Taylor's Island store.

For those of us born to the automobile it is virtually impossible to understand what the steamboat meant in an area of water-imposed isolation. It brought the first comfortable, reliable year-round transportation to people who had been dependent on the vagaries of wind and sail. It was no wonder they revered her memory.

The Emma Giles was just one of many steamboats that sailed out of Baltimore. The era has been captured in *Steamboats out of Baltimore* by Robert H. Burgess and H.

Graham Wood (copyright1968, by Tidewater Publishers, a Division of Cornell Maritime Press, Inc.). These two gentlemen were caught up in a life-long enthusiasm for boats on the Bay. Here is how they dedicated their book:

"To those who as children, or even as adults, thrilled at the nightly parade of snow-white steamboats out of Baltimore, caught in the slanting golden rays of a setting sun; who stood enthralled on the freight deck and peered into the engine room and heard the ker-chee, ker-chaw of steam from the machinery as the walking beam rocked to and fro; who listened from their stateroom berths to the cries throughout the night of the sheep and calves one deck below, or to the slap of the paddle wheels on the surface of the water and the sound of a bell buoy fading astern; to those who recall with nostalgia the unmatched, pleasant aroma of a steamboat's interior; who heard the clarion sound of the steam whistle blowing for a landing in the quiet, early morning hours; and to those who waited on a country wharf for what seemed like hours before sighting the smoke and then the steamer's stack over the trees around the next bend and have never forgotten the spell of it all, this book is dedicated."

Friends I made in Dorchester county had often "waited on a country wharf" for the *Emma Giles* to take them out of their humdrum routines and into the excitement of the big city. They came aboard with the picnic lunches they had packed at home and enjoyed them on deck to "the slap of the paddle wheel." Fifty cents for a meal in the dining room was a little steep for cash-strapped country folk. As dark fell and Baltimore approached, they waited for the pungent fragrance of McCormick's spice factory to greet them. Sometimes it almost overpowered the nearby fertilizer plant as the steamboat snubbed into her berth at Pier 11, Light Street, around 11 p.m.

In her heyday, the *Emma Giles* stopped at Taylor's Island twice a week on Tuesdays and Thursdays, having left her berth in Baltimore between 6 and 7 in the morning. She was expected to arrive at the Island in time to load freight and passengers and be on her way to her other stops by noon. So when Hester Neild heard her mother call, "Hattie, run up to the attic and watch for the *Emma Giles,* now, you hear. I'm waiting for a new dress pattern," the four-year-old, full of importance, would tear up the steps to the stuffy attic, and watch out the window. She might hear the "clarion sound of the steam whistle" before the boat came in sight and run downstairs, calling "Mama, mama she's coming. Let's hurry." After Taylor's Island the *Emma Giles* headed for Milton Wharf at Woolford, Spedden's Wharf on the opposite shore of the Little Choptank River (called the Neck District) and on to Lowe's Wharf which nobody seems to remember, before returning to Baltimore. All that travel for only 25 cents

Emma, the little girl whose name this beloved steamboat bore, was the only daughter of the man who advanced the funds for her construction. She christened the shiny new vessel with a bottle of champagne in Baltimore in 1887. Her portrait in oils hung at the foot of a red-carpeted stairway. For country folk, such splendor, such elegance was a sight never to be forgotten.

Much about the *Emma Giles* was unique. The round pilot house, for one thing and the wooden cover for her paddle wheel, decorated with a carving of a beehive with bees surrounded by flowers. Most such covers bore a carved American eagle.

In 1920 the *Emma Giles* cut her trips down to once a week, making the same stops as before, but less often. It was the handwriting on the wall. The automobile had become the transportation of choice. Fewer and fewer passengers took the steamboat. In 1924 she was taken off the Little Choptank run and sent to the upper Bay.

Cutting their cloth to fit the shape of a new day, the steamboat companies converted some of their boats to automobile ferries as visitors from the western shore flocked to Tolchester's beach and its amusement park.

The Messrs Burgess and Wood tell us the sad news that by 1936 the upper Bay routes had been abandoned and "the *Emma Giles had* her freight deck opened at the bow to enable her to carry automobiles." It was an indignity she would not long survive. In 1939 she was converted to a barge.

But in the hearts of the passengers who remembered her glory days, she would always be their dreamboat steamboat.

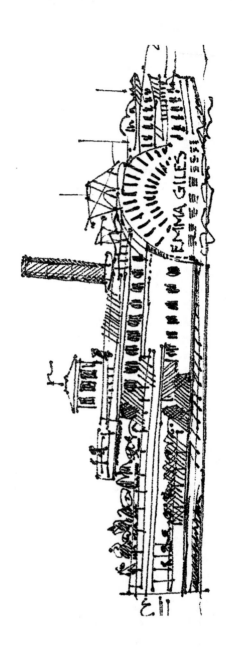

The 20th Century -- Up Tempo

At the dawn of the 20th century the tempo of life on Taylor's Island matched that of the steamboats on the Bay and the clip-clop of horses' hooves.

Yes, soon automobiles driven by Duncan Noble and Staplefort Neild went break necking down roads at 25 miles per hour, scaring the wits out of man and beast. Even a young daredevil who had learned to fly during World War One landed a seaplane on Slaughter Creek and crashed when he tried to take off. He was unharmed; parts of the plane salvaged from the water were stored in one of Staplefort Neild's barns and forgotten. History's leftovers lived in those barns.

Though the World War I song asked: "How Ya Gonna Keep 'Em Down on the Farm, after they've Seen Paree?" the local Doughboys came home and stayed home.

Though the pace was picking up everywhere else, on Taylor's Island 20-20 vision and a magnifying glass could hardly detect a trend. Here change collided with inertia and met defeat. "That's the way we've always done it," carried the day.

Though an operator asked "Number, please?" when you cranked your phone, and connected you to a party line, progress was not always welcome. When the Rural Electrification Administration in the post World War II years, proposed bringing electricity to the Island, one woman dug in her heels and refused to allow any poles to be set up on her property. You can see her, arms akimbo, defying progress with the spunk of a Molly Pitcher.

The automobile, aside. The Briggs & Stratton engines in the watermen's boats, aside. Life flowed slowly, quietly, untroubled by intrusive news broadcasts in the absence of radios. The pace of life on Taylor's Island was geared more to rising and falling tides and the cycles of the seasons.

Isolation, too, played a big role. The Choptank River neatly splits the Eastern Shore of Maryland in two. A look at a map shows how cleanly the southern half is cut off. But cut off from what?

Life on a farm provided all a family's needs except salt, sugar, coffee and baking powder. Laura Robinson Navy, who was born and reared on Taylor's Island, waxed lyrical about the abundance of fine victuals available on her father's farm when she was a girl in the early 1900s.

As an older woman she wrote:

"Where in the world could you eat better?

"The marshlands proved good grazing for cattle and the salt in the marsh grass gave the milk and butter we produced a superior flavor.

"I can think of many wonderful things from the land and the water. Fish, oysters, clams were plentiful. We had chicken and turkey. Guinea fowl was a must.

"Trapping muskrats in winter was both a source of food and profit. Marsh rabbit, as we called it, was considered a delicious dish.

"There was terrapin and the old bull turtle, for a pie.

"Not forgetting ducks, geese and plain old rabbit."

Cut off from what?

Spring peepers announced the beginning of warm weather. The redwing blackbirds nested in the reeds. The mosquitoes rose in blinding clouds; tomatoes ripened; soybeans dried in the fields and rattled in the autumn breeze. Snow covered the ground, sending the deer to nibble tender growth on young fruit trees. The earth circled the sun. The moon rose over the water in a sky unsullied by city lights. Venus shone brightly before the sky was fully dark, and the stars appeared in the thousands as the night deepened. In the distance a lonely whippoorwill called.

Cut off from what?

"The Bread House"

Her long braids flying, her wet cotton dress hiked up above her knees, Laura Robinson liked to ride out into the shallows astride one of her father's horses and wave to the passengers lined up along the rail of the *Emma Giles*. And then spin around and gallop back home. Bareback.

The Robinson farm lay on Holland Point at the extreme northeastern corner of Taylor's Island, and the *Emma Giles* would stop there to take on freight if the captain saw a flag hoisted at the wharf -- a signal that there was produce to ship to Baltimore. Laura remembered, "usually there'd be fruit, or eggs, or poultry to load, but sometimes there'd be a lamb or a calf." Farmers were grateful not to have to cart their wares all the way down to the landing by the bridge over the muddy roads. Laura often told about the time she arrived at school one day with mud splashed on her hat. "All the way up onto my hat."

The farm provided all the meat the family ate during the winter and vegetables for the table and for canning. The Mason jars of canned tomatoes and string beans and corn and peas lined the pantry shelves in colorful profusion. The trees bore apples and peaches and pears for jams and jellies. And the peppers and cucumbers were made into piccalilli, relishes, and sweet pickles. And it produced all the flour and all the lard Laura's mother used to bake the quantities of bread needed to feed the family and the farm hands.

Laura's mother used up 12 or 13 barrels of flour every year. And when a barrel held between 165 and 185 pounds of flour, it's clear that Mrs. Robinson mixed up, kneaded and baked at least a ton of flour a year. Laura said their place came to be known as "The Bread House."

Bread, on Taylor's Island, did not mean loaves baked from yeast-risen dough. Rather, bread was baked from biscuit dough, a mixture of flour and lard, baking powder and a pinch of salt, moistened with clabber and kneaded until it was just right. What was just right? Only the hands of the experienced baker knew by feel when the dough was elastic and lustrous enough for the oven.

Mrs. Robinson baked her bread in big round loaves, ten inches across, in the lids of lard tins. She could bake eight lids of bread at a time in the wood stove. Laura liked to be on hand when it came out of the oven, hot and flaky, and smear a chunk with gobs of farm-churned butter and homemade blackberry jam.

Meanwhille, on the other side of the Island near Oyster Cove, Bill Keene was transplanting young tomato plants and setting out corn seedlings for ten cents an hour. At 12 or 13, he was putting in ten hours a day. But it was not all toil and sweat. There were rewards. He got to ride on the old Mogol tractor. As a successful elderly gentleman, Bill could still remember the sound of the one-cylinder engine going 'bloop, bloop, bloop' as she hiccupped along. "How the other boys envied me, sitting there high up on the seat of that old tractor. Bloop . . . bloop . . . bloop."

Summers, Bill worked in the wheat field. And at harvest time, it was his job to make neat bundles of wheat straw and stuff them into sacks. All for a dollar a day. Saturdays, though, he worked only half-day.

The farm belonged to Mr. Jim Spicer who lived at Mulberry Grove, the oldest house on the Island. A story goes with Mulberry Grove and you will hear it later.

When Bill wasn't working for Mr. Spicer he might be out shooting hawks. Hawks were predators that swooped down and raided the chicken farms. He could collect a bounty of 50 cents for every hawk beak he took in to Constable Goehegan. Some days he could clear between $6 and $8 when the hawks were migrating. He had a favorite spot beside a pine tree where he would stake out a position and when the flocks flew over he'd blast away, until sometimes, he admitted, "my gun barrel got hot." And he was not the only boy out looking to pick up a few dollars in bounty money.

He liked to tell the story about how his father once got mistaken for his mother. A neighbor working in his garden some distance from the Keene house, saw a figure in a long skirt come out the door with a shotgun, blast a hawk out of the sky, toss it aside and pop back inside, all in the blink of an eye. Soon a story a making the rounds that Mrs. Keene -- such a nice little lady -- was a regular Annie Oakley. In fact, it was Bill's father, laid up with the grippe, which heard a ruckus in his chicken yard, jumped from bed, his long nightshirt flapping around his ankles, and bagged the bird.

Bill went to the Oyster Creek School, a one-room building later relegated to use as storage. On Saturdays he and a friend might bicycle into Cambridge to see a movie. The show would include a newsreel, selections from coming attractions, a segment of a serial, and, finally, the main feature. The whole thing could last for three hours, and the boys were free to sit through two performances if they wanted to.

The trip to town by bicycle took close to two-hours. So when the time came to start high school in Cambridge, Bill was happy to accept a ride in Staplefort Neild's Model T Ford with flaps on the side to keep out the rain. If they made good time, they could pick up friends along the way and be at the schoolhouse within an hour.

At 19, after graduating, Bill boarded the *Emma Giles* heading for Baltimore to seek his fortune.

The young men who stayed behind found entertainment on the sandy beaches and dance pavilions along the shores of Chesapeake Bay. There were two pavilions, one at the now-vanished Punch Island at the southernmost tip of Taylor's Island and another one, described as being "near the old Carpenter place by Oyster Cove." A five-mile walk to reach a dance was commonplace; eight wasn't too far.

Sometimes an accordion supplied the music. Sometimes Charlie Creighton played his fiddle. Couples danced the fox trot to the strains of "Whispering" and "Avalon" and "Ramona" and other favorites of the day. In winter, dances were held in different homes, with families taking turns hosting the parties where ham biscuits and fried chicken abounded.

No wonder Bill Keene sometimes got homesick, up there all by himself in the big city.

Homemakers

Mabel Neild, Staplefort's wife, was putting up straw-
berries when Hattie Brookes of the Extension Service knocked
on her kitchen door. "Mabel," Hattie said in her quiet but
persuasive way, "I want you to come to the Rural Women's
meeting in College Park this year."

"Oh, I can't," Mabel, said at once. "I just can't." And kept
on hulling berries.

Hattie persisted. "Your son is old enough now to be left
alone and I'm sure your husband and he can get along without
you for a few days. Now don't say no to me until you've
talked it over with Staplefort."

The upshot was that Mabel Neild went on the first of many
trips to a Rural Womens' Short Course on the campus of the
University of Maryland, a program instituted in 1923.

In its early years, "bus loads of women converged on the
University campus. Not too many families had cars, and even a
ride on a bus was an event," Jeanette Green, a historian of
Extension Homemaking wrote[8]   (Don't forget -- there was still
no bridge over the Choptank River at Cambridge at that time.)

The campus atmosphere had a heady effect.   The women
shed inhibitions, kicked up their heels, played tricks on each
other like college girls and had a wonderful time. Aware of this
tendency, their mentors set aside a time each day to write a
letter home, assuring the family that mother was all right.

For women of that time, lacking the freedom to hop in the
family car and run down to the supermarket, the fresh air of
change gave their lives new meaning and quality.   They
enjoyed sightseeing tours of Washington, D. C., and once a
group traveled by "chartered streetcars to the Seventh Street
wharf where they boarded a boat for a trip to Mt. Vernon." A

---

[8] "Today's Home Builds Tomorrow's World", Researched and Written
by Jeanette Green, Extension Homemaker, 1982.
A mimeographed history of the "Neck District Extension Homemakers' Club
History - 1920 - 1983" by Hilda Lee Marshall.   (The aptly-named Neck
District sticks out into the Little Choptank River.)

trip down the Potomac on the steamboat *Charles Macalester* was a prized outing for anyone in Washington, D.C.

Jeanette Green's account notes with pride that no other state had such a program. She calls it a "two-way road" where Information and guidance flowed out and problems, and solutions developed by the folks back home, flowed back in return, and had "their influence upon the land grant college and the United States Department of Agriculture."

Back home, at meetings of their local chapters, the women got together to talk about things like butchering hogs and cleaning chickens. But they talked about making sherbet, too -- "if any of the members could get some ice," and the discussion next time might deal with "Corsets and their Relation to Health."

Hattie Brookes, who had come to Dorchester County with the Extension Service in 1926 and stayed for 33 years, touched and shaped the lives of hundreds of women. And she endured forever in their memories.

Throughout her life, Mabel Neild continued to participate in Dorchester County Homemakers' activities and rose to positions of prominence.

The Taylor's Island Club was an active one, holding monthly meetings. A longtime president was Patsy Carpenter, wife of Reynolds, a prominent Island resident. Patsy had literally grown up in the organization. When she was a little girl she had gone to meetings in Cambridge with her mother and this early interest never left her. She remained a dedicated Homemaker and was widely famous throughout Dorchester County for her cakes, as delicious as they were beautifully decorated.

Under Patsy's leadership, the June Homemakers meeting was held in the Chapel of Ease, honoring Senator George Radcliffe's wish that it be used by the people of Taylor's Island.

Hooch

Prohibition, as a topic of conversation, never ever arose -- not even among the men who sat on the bench down the middle of the Big Store and swigged beer out of bottles concealed in a brown paper bags. Secrets were kept.

The 18th Amendment to the Constitution which prohibited the making or sale of alcoholic beverages went into effect in 1919 and lasted until 1933 when the 21st amendment repealed it

Although I never heard any mention of rum running or smuggling, a first-hand account follows, thanks to our brief experience with a little magazine.

A friend of my husband -- I'll call him John -- had long dreamed of starting a magazine. A publication with a local focus appealed to him, and he bought from an enterprising young woman named Lyn Lewis a freebie she had started called *Combing the Shores*. It circulated in an area between Easton and Salisbury.

John renamed it *Shore Lines*. My husband and I were happy to play along and offer whatever skills we had. A Cambridge bank offered us office space, free, and we set up shop. We had no computer -- indeed, computers were a few years in the future.

The first issue bore the date February, 1979. John worked hard to recruit writers, which he found heavy going, and I tried to sell advertising. The job held no appeal to me.

The last issue of *Shore Lines* was dated June, 1979, and it carried a story by a Taylor's Islander named Milton Shenton (no relation to Robert Shenton who owned the store). Milton had found fame as the first American G.I. to enter Paris at the end of World War II.

But the story he tells here takes place at a time when "rum runners" sold imported liquor to "bootleggers" who supplied "speakeasies" where cocktails were often served in teacups to camouflage their real identity.

Here's Milton's story.

"He's My Eyes, Cap'n"
By Milton M. Shenton

The boy came awake instantly. Without moving a muscle he lay listening. Something unnatural, some sound had interrupted his slumber. Climbing quietly out of bed, he moved across the room on bare feet and pressed an ear against the wall. Mother and father were arguing . . .

Mack wasn't quite 11 years old and would be in sixth grade come September. Small but wiry, he was the second of three children born to Joseph and LaVerne. Father was a waterman. Although money was hard to come by, a big garden furnished vegetables by the bushel, and turkeys, geese and chickens roamed the yard. Hogs were always in the pens. A cow furnished milk and butter, and acres of woodland furnished the house with heat.

No electricity, no phone, no running water, and best of all, no mortgage payments. This was the world that Mack, an older sister and a two-year-old brother grew up into. His little brother took to him like a tick to a hound, and they romped for hours.

But Mack's greatest love was his father's boat. A 40=-footer, she was a workhorse of a boat -- big, powered by a Fairbanks Morse engine originally bought in New York by one of father's fishing friends. She was made to order for pulling scows loaded with trap poles and seine boats loaded with nets. Mack couldn't keep his hands off that boat, and being able to actually stop and reverse quickly was something out of this world. Steering lines went completely around the boat and connected with a steering stick just aft of the motor.

Every chance he got, Mack followed Pop out on the boat. And Pop responded by teaching the boy everything he knew.

"Son, always respect the wind and the water," Pop told him again and again. These were words the boy never forgot.

Like most boys growing up, Mack got into trouble on occasion, as when his mother caught him smoking behind the turkey house. Now LaVerne was a large woman, 165 pounds, and strong as an ox. Also she was left-handed (not that this mattered much.)

She'd tell the boy, "Now, son, I've got to punish you and even thought it hurts me more than you (he doubted this) give me your hand." Her right hand would clamp on his skinny wrist and then would begin his little dance. Round and round with the switch tearing at those dancing legs . . .

As he listened, Mack realized he was the subject of the argument. Mother said, "I will not stand for it. He's too small and if something should happen we could never live with ourselves."

Pressing his ear closer, he heard Pop say, "But they've asked for my boat and he'd only have to steer in the Bay. You know I don't see very well in the dark, and that boy has eyes like a owl.

"Then there's the money. . . more than I can make in a month fishing. We do need the money badly and I'll promise nothing will happen to the boy."

As he slid back into bed, Mack smiled. He knew there'd be no more sleep for him this night, and he knew too that his mother would relent. She trusted Pop completely. After all, wasn't Pop the absolutely best waterman anywhere around? If only he had night vision.

But God had blessed Mack with exceptional eyesight at night and a sort of built-in dead reckoning.

Curling into a ball, Mack tried to anticipate the events that awaited him. He knew he'd soon embark upon a great adventure. He was going to become a rumrunner.

The 40-footer nosed out of the mouth at the top of Inlet Island and turned southwest. Her bow lifted slightly in the Bay's gentle swell. Standing on a box, the boy peered intently into the darkness. No running lights showed and the night seemed to envelop his father standing braced on the cabin top.

Off to starboard, miles away, Bluff Point light blinked palely. The Fairbanks Morse engine purred like a kitten.

Mack kept one hand on the stick and the other close to the controls. He'd made many trips with his father, but tonight was something special. He had to steer a southwest course and locate another boat lying at anchor -- completely blacked out -- somewhere in this big Bay!

Because he knew he had to return this way, Mack kept an

anxious eye over his shoulder. The sky was dark, and only a few stars shone through. Over his left shoulder was a cluster of three in a triangular pattern and if they didn't fade, Mack knew they would be a good reference point coming back. Atop the cabin, his father was restless.

Maybe this was too big a chore for the lad! Maybe he should have listened to LaVerne. Anyway, he was committed now and maybe the kid could pull it off.

"Do you see anything yet?" he'd ask.

"No, sir. But I'll find them, don't worry."

Out quite a ways now and suddenly there was a blur ahead. The boy swings his eyes side to side and slightly upward. Never looking directly at it, he makes out an object. Whispering and pointing, he tells his father he thinks this is the rendezvous.

Now Pop is really nervous.

"You know what to do, son. Can you handle it?"

"Yes, sir. I got this end, you handle the rest of the deal."

"Ahoy, Cap'n. You got a name?"

Pop calls back: "Yes, sir. This is the *Victoria* out of Inlet Island. We've wandered off course and could you give us some instructions?"

Mack knew this was the prearranged signal.

"All right, Cap'n. Come alongside. We'll talk."

"Can you dock her all right, son?"

Eagerly now, Mack tells him. "Yes, sir. I'll guarantee I've got this end."

Easing upwind, hitting reverse, catching her on the swing, then putting the *Vic* alongside as gently as a mother's caress.

"Where'd that Gawd damn kid come from?"

Pop answers: "It's all right, Cap'n. That's my son and he's my eyes."

The *Wild Rose,* 60 feet of pure power. High flaring bow with a rake back aft that bespeaks the tremendous speed of three Packard motors.

But Mack doesn't have much time to admire her. Boiling on deck comes the crew. Eight or 10 men, each brandishing a Thompson Sub or sawed-off shotgun.

Mack knew these 60-footers were built especially for this

job. They went into the ocean down off the Capes and unloaded the ships that smuggled the hooch in from foreign ports -- ships that lay just outside the Limits and waited to transfer their cargo to the small, speedy 60-footers.

They, in turn, were unloaded by local watermen -- men who knew every cove, inlet, sandbar and deserted wharf and who could be trusted to keep their mouths shut, especially after being paid a fat fee for their services.

This was how Pop and the *Vic* had become involved.

Pop is explaining to the captain about how his eyes are bad and how his son did the steering. How tight-mouthed the boy was, in fact, tight as a clam. How he'd give them his word of honor the boy would die before he'd talk.

"O.K.," the captain says. "One peep out of the kid and it'll be deep six for both of you."

Mack remembered reading *Moby Dick* and *Treasure Island*. He shuddered. Maybe Blackbeard was back on the Bay!

Loading the Vic with cases wrapped in burlap didn't take long and the order to cast off was given. Once away, Mack turned toward Inlet Island.

Pop was quiet now, standing on the cabin. Hunkered down beside him was an armed guard.

The Fairbanks Morse purred on.

Heading northeast now, and Mack struggled with his thoughts. Got to find Inlet Island. Suppose he ran the *Vic* aground and the sun came up on them? He wondered if those guys would really "deep six" him.

Find that cluster of stars and steer directly on. The night seemed darker now, and Pop was restless again.

"Are you all right, son?"

"Yes, sir. I got her. Be hitting the mouth of that Inlet pretty soon now."

How he wished he felt that sure. The shoreline was just one black continuous and unbroken line. The boy searched desperately for something to identify his location. And he found it.

Not uttering a sound he swung the bow southeast and headed into the mouth. Noting the change in direction, Pop was instantly alert and asking, "Is this it?"

"Yes, sir. We'll be at the bridge in a few minutes."

The guard stirred and murmured something. Pop told him he never doubted for one minute that the youngster could find the mouth.

"Now, son, you got a flood tide. Think you can put 'er through that big span?"

"Yes, sir."

The bridge loomed dark and low. Seemed not enough room to pass under.

Now Pop was walking the washboard.

"Easy, son. Go through the wide span in the channel.

"Yes, sir. I got 'er."

The boy skimmed through the span just like a chimney swallow.

Tying up at the pier and unloading is just routine for the boy now. A big truck looms out of the darkness, with more armed guards and evidently the top wheel, Big Ben. The guard on the *Vic* jumps ashore and greets Big Ben with a gush of praise for this squirt of a kid that had to stand on a brick to kiss a duck in the ... How the kid could see in the dark and handle a boat as if he'd grown up on it. And how maybe Big Ben ought to take the boy up to New York with him.

And Pop saying how this kid is all he's got and there ain't enough money in the world to buy him. Maybe they were joshing, but anyway Mack stands there 10 feet tall at that moment. He's also doing something Pop had often told him: "Now son, no matter what you see, keep your mouth shut and your eyes open."

Back home in his bed -- it was still dark and dawn some hours away -- Mack lay wide-awake. With a thrill of pride he thought back over the discussion about taking him up to New York.

But most of all he thought about his mother. The tears welled up in her eyes when he came through the kitchen door. She grabbed him and hugged him fiercely and rocked him in her arms. And when his father came in, turned to him and said: "There! I knew he could do it. I never had a moment's doubt. I just knew he could do it!"

66

Distance Bridged -- October 26, 1935

It was a day for unbridled celebration. It was a day like none before -- or none after. It was the day the Emerson Harrington bridge across the Choptank River at Cambridge opened for traffic.

President Franklin D. Roosevelt came down for its dedication, bringing Senator George Radcliffe, Democrat of Maryland, as his guest aboard the yacht *Sequoia.*

A young reporter for the Cambridge *Daily Banner* named Elsie McNamara, clutching her tickets for seats in the reviewing stand, had trouble making her way through the traffic and the crowds. In an interview with the *Baltimore Sun* forty years later, her memories of the occasion were still vivid.

It was a bright, blue October day; a light breeze ruffled the waters; the sun struck sparks from the waves. Cambridge burned with excitement. On the Choptank River hundreds of boats of all sizes -- rowboats, sailboats, workboats and cabin cruisers -- jostled for a place where they could catch a glimpse of President Roosevelt.

Emerson C. Harrington, one of Dorchester County's own who had served as Governor of Maryland from 1916 to 1920, was a long-time advocate of a bridge connecting Cambridge with the Talbot County side of the river. Born in Madison -- once called Tobacco Stick -- his brother Benjamin had founded the Harrington Canning Factory on Taylor's Island.

Reporter McNamara remembers that President Roosevelt "crippled by polio, never left the Sequoia. He leaned upon the ship railing as he delivered a short speech in a soft voice."

The draw span on the bridge was opened; the *Sequoia* sailed up the river through it, swung back around returning on the Talbot County side of the river and headed home to Washington.

At about 3 o'clock that afternoon, local traffic began moving, for the first time, across the Choptank River from Cambridge to Talbot County's shore. Slowly, slowly, creaking like an old batten door on strap hinges rusty with disuse, Dorchester County began to open up.

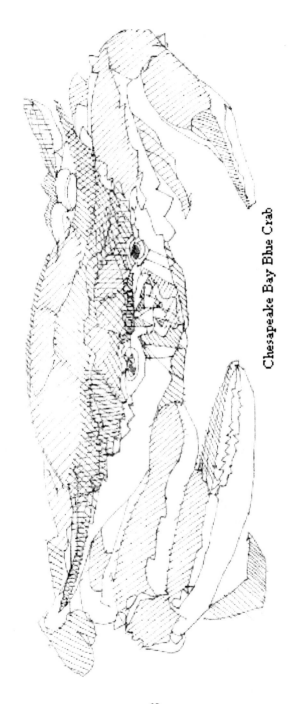

Chesapeake Bay Blue Crab

Electric

It is 1947. Christmas, 1947. Bobby Spicer is humming "Joy to the World" as she trims her Christmas tree. Now the last ball is hung. The tinsel is in place. The Big Moment has arrived. She plugs the lights into a long extension cord and makes Taylor's Island history in five colors.

Bobby was a Baltimore girl who met handsome Travers Spicer during World War II when he was in the Coast Guard. They fell in love, married, and Bobby came to Taylor's Island as a bride to a house with outdoor plumbing and kerosene lamps. But she brought her collection of Christmas decorations with her and waited. Then in 1947, that memorable year, she finally strung her tree with lights. It was a time for joy.

Cambridge had had electricity since 1900. It's hard to credit that it took almost 50 years for the wires to stretch those 20 miles. Without the Rural Electrification Administration, a New Deal agency formed to bring electricity into areas too remote and too unprofitable for private companies to bother with, it could have taken even longer to juice up the Island. And even then there had been a few who were "agin' the electric", as they called it. They were shouted down.

By 1948 World War II was a thing of the past. Factories had stopped making guns and tanks and started turning out the appliances Americans had been thirsting for -- refrigerators and washing machines and stoves and electric fans. Bobby Spicer, city girl, was quick to embrace it. But for many people, committed to their old ways, change came gradually. However, when your next-door neighbor installed his electric pump, it could be humiliating to go out to the well for your own water.

Cooks grown used to woodstoves and wise to their vagaries, were slow to part with them. The new electric stoves were hard to figure out and tricky to use. But come summertime, everybody had to admit that with an electric stove the kitchen was a whole lot cooler and those new electric fans sure stirred up a nice breeze!

Mason jars and the rite of canning   in the heat of late August gradually gave way to the new freezers. Washtubs and washboards were   relegated to the barn, replaced by washing machines. Dryers got the go-by. You just can't beat hanging clothes on the line to dry in the sun. Electric hot water heaters had demonstrated that the Saturday night bath could be a downright luxury. However, the old cesspools were not equipped to handle the amount of water that flowed out of bath tubs and they tended to overflow. On the other hand, installing a septic system could run awfully high.

Cambridge hardware stores for the first time   found men from Taylor's Island roaming the aisles looking at the power tools and wondering how on earth anybody had ever built boats with nothing but hand saws!

Electric light exerted a universal appeal and within a short time few homes were without, at the very least, a 40-watt bulb dangling   by a cloth-insulated wire from the kitchen ceiling. The lowly light bulb, itself, created an unanticipated hazard. But we won't talk about that yet.

Distance Shrinks – July 1952

In July, 1952, a bridge across the Chesapeake Bay opened. It was a dream come true for travelers to the Eastern Shore who had once spent hours in hot cars waiting for slow ferries. Several years passed before the array of fast food restaurants, shopping centers, and bait stores sprang up on either end of the bridge. In the early days, from Annapolis to Easton was a straight shot down a dark road.

Our family -- my husband Joe, our daughter Mary, aged three, and I --crossed this bridge together for the first time in April, 1960, on a trip to find a house on the water where we could spend weekends and summer vacations, as well as those two-month long holidays called "home leave" by members of the United States diplomatic corps.

Affordability was the Number One factor. I had in the back of my mind a price of $7,500, which I secretly suspected was unrealistic. Joe had in mind a drive that would take, at most, two hours. I realized my dream. He settled for a three-hour drive.

We found an old farm house on an island, fully furnished, ready to move into, offering hot and cold running water and a bathtub with feet. Without asking too many questions -- we were naive city folks, innocent about pumps and wells and cesspools -- we bought it.

On the drive from Cambridge out to Taylor's Island, a trip of some 20 miles, the real estate agent filled us in on some of the local lore. He pointed out a rise believed to be an Indian mound where arrowheads and other artifacts had been found. He told us the legend that Dorchester County's shore line, alone, exceeded that of the entire United States.

And as we neared the house, driving down a dirt road, he told us that in bad weather it could be difficult. "Along about here, most people want to turn back," he said. We laughed and told him we had spent a number of years driving around the back roads of Yugoslavia and were not intimidated.

71

Our first view of the house -- the back.

Front view -- from photo furnished by Matthews &
Company, 6 Poplar Street, Cambridge,MD.
This side faced Slaughter Creek.

The House

The   house rose, sad and solitary, at the end of a long rutted lane.   It occupied a gentle rise -- local people called it a hill -- thirty or forty yards back from the water's edge.

An old farm house, it was composed of three sections spliced together, in the fashion of houses on the Eastern Shore. There, moving houses was no unusual event. If the Bay had nibbled your front yard down to a nubbin, it was time to move the house back, possibly even to relocate it.

This house occupied an acre of ground surrounded on three sides by a barbed wire fence overgrown with honeysuckle vines intertwined with wild blackberry.   A pier jutted out into the water of Slaughter Creek where a heavy growth of water grass along the shoreline defied any idea of wading or swimming. There were also a corncrib; a woodshed and a building called a garage built, it was clear, to house a Model A Ford, nothing larger.

The kitchen windows betrayed some age. The glass in the six over six lights was splotched with small bubbles the size of rice grains and had a faint greenish tinge.   Or was this a reflection of the green vinyl squares that covered the kitchen floor, the sickly green paint covering the beaverboard walls and the perilously low ceiling?

The center section, however, was truly a centerpiece. A graceful room, its tall windows were furnished with 12 over 6 lights; there were two doors, one facing east toward the water, the other west, overlooking four ancient mulberry trees and some farmland.

The fireplace breast of beaded pine paneling had been heavily daubed with white paint, and the bricks surrounding the firebox had started to crumble.   The random-width floorboards hid beneath countless coats of gray paint. The high ceiling was, curiously, painted the same dark green as the walls above the simple chair rail, and threatened to fall.   But its finely - balanced proportions gave the room an indestructible elegance. The ceiling, however, was painted dark green, a mystery.

Curling behind the fireplace, a short flight of steps, narrow, curving and steep, rose to a bedroom above, following a pattern familiar to the shipbuilders who turned their hand to building houses.

In the rear, like a stepchild, was yet another room, so crowded by a double bed, a gigantic kerosene space heater, and the lower half of a clumsy flight of steps, that there was barely room to walk through. There were no closets. A nail in the wall had sufficed for overalls and aprons.

The room above it was clearly an afterthought. It was larger than the room below, making for an overhang.

We bought this house in 1960. It was furnished with an eclectic assortment of furnishings ranging from pots and pans to sagging beds with rusty springs and lumpy cotton mattresses. The seats of the kitchen chairs were covered with imitation leather from which excelsior stuffing tried here and there to escape.

A great many people, some long dead, some still alive, had lived there. They had battled hordes of aggressive mosquitoes in summer, managed against all odds to keep warm in winter. And they had left behind vestiges of themselves.

Behind some wainscoting, a long-lost button hook -- that obsolete gadget so essential in coaxing small cylindrical shoe buttons through stubborn leathern holes.

A spool serving as a door pull on a screen door -- it had once held Clarks ONT thread, had been designed by some long-gone technical genius to perch on the spindle of a sewing machine and pay out its thread without snarl or hitch. And when these spools were empty, children used them to blow soap bubbles; carpenters used them as handy door pulls.

A mysterious hole in the paneled door leading from the kitchen to the great room, artfully patched over with the lid of a coffee can. The job captured our respect and admiration. What was behind the patch? Why had a hole been made?

A notch cut into a chair rail, perhaps by a small boy trying out his new pocketknife.

Even a warm and welcoming smell compounded of bread baking in a long-gone oven, mice behind the baseboards, mildew and dried sage -- an amalgam of a century of living.

While I lived in the house I was never tempted to tamper with these signatures of the men and women who had gone before. Even as we made improvements, I respected them. When a contractor removed the patched door, my husband and I both insisted he bring that door back, and rehang it. "B-b-b-but," he spluttered, "it's got that patch on it."

"Yes," we said in unison, "Yes. Exactly the point. Bring it back. Now!"

Time wields a wide and swift eraser. Before all memory of the people who once lived in this old house has vanished like an island in the Bay, I would like to capture what I learned about them and how they lived.

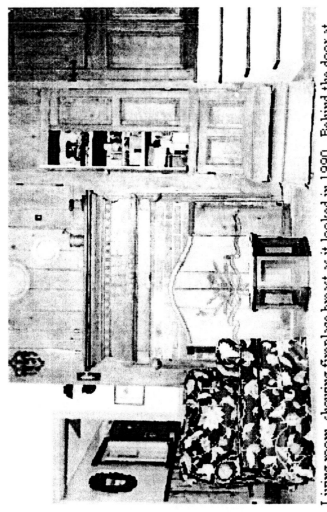

Living room, showing fireplace breast as it looked in 1990. Behind the door at the right, the stairs continue to wind upward to the bedroom above.

Ghosts

His name, alone, qualifies William Staplefort for a footnote in history.   He was descended from Raymond Stapleforte, the first sheriff of Dorchester County, and the original document from Lord Baltimore charging him   to "call a special election of members to sit in the colonial assembly, thus establishing [Dorchester] county . . ." remained in family hands on Taylor's Island.

William, though married, made the mistake of falling in love with Laura, about whom we know little except that she lived off the Island.

He divorced his wife and married Laura.   Under Methodist church law, divorce was not recognized then, and the church records show that   "William Staplefort returned to the world." "Written out of the church," his grandson, Staplefort had once explained to me.

The couple came to live in the house when its amenities included little more than a well, an outhouse and woodstoves. Cracks between the floorboards served as vents to circulated frigid air in winter.   But in summer, their grandchildren, Hester and Staplefort Neild, had loved to visit the house when they were small and they told me what they remembered.

Hester, a portly woman in her seventies when I knew her, had been principal of a school in Cambridge.   Grown men who had gone to her school remembered Miss Hester for her generosity with the ruler.   She told me there had once been   a gazebo down by the water's edge where she had played with her dolls.   And fifty years later, from the oozy mud where the gazebo had once stood, I   found the China shards of a doll's head and a small porcelain hand that had once hung from the stuffed arm of a Victorian doll.

In the usage of a by-gone day, she called Staplefort "Brother."   "Brother" told me of a scientific experiment he had carried out down by the barn when he was ten years old, or so, and boys believed you could find out if   a snake had legs by holding it over a fire.   "Now don't you ever tell this," he admonished me, a man past sixty, "but once I caught a snake up in the loft of the barn. An old mother cat lived up there and they say that snakes like milk and sometimes sneak in and suckle a mother cat.

"I caught a snake, not a very big one, and held it over a little fire. Now don't you tell I did that," he said, in mock seriousness.

"And," I asked, "Did the snake have legs?"

With a wicked grin, he answered: "Why don't you try it for yourself and see?"

William suffered a heart attack in his skiff and was found dead and adrift on Slaughter Creek around the turn of the 20th century. Laura lived with Mabel and Staplefort Neild until her death.

# # #

Newlyweds, Olin Horseman and his bride Mabel, moved into the house in the early years of the 20th Century. Mabel Horseman bore four or five children there. She and Olin were cousins, and the local people allowed that some of their children were "not right bright." Olin once told us how one of his young sons announced that he was going to walk across Slaughter Creek, at that point about a third of a mile wide. Olin watched as the little fellow trudged out into the shallows, feet on the bottom, and kept on walking until the water was almost over his head, when Olin ran out and saved him.

I learned many years later that an infant daughter had died in the house. Maggie Phillips, nee Horseman -- it was a big family -- paid a visit to the house. She sat on the screen porch with her sister and me, sipping iced tea and munching cookies. Maggie was an untaught artist whose primitives were much admired by her neighbors, although her sales were negligible. She wore her jet-black hair in a pre-Raphaelite part down the middle and exuded an aura of other worldliness. If you had seen her strolling down the road, leading a Maurice Sendak dwarf by either hand, you would not have been surprised.

"I can see her now," Maggie said, nodding toward the small sofa in the great room. "Lying there so peaceful in death. Her little pinkie curled like that. " Maggie curled her own pinkie. "Oh, how I'd love to paint that picture. Poor little sweet baby..."

And her sister, a woman whose feet stood flat on the ground, interrupted. "Oh Maggie, hush up. Miss Frances won't get a wink of sleep in this house again if you keep that up."

Olin Horseman was a boat builder. He had no access to power tools on Taylor's Island at that time. Every plank was sawed by hand, ever hole bored with a hand drill. Staplefort had suggested to us that a sunken skiff down beside the pier was probably one Olin had built and might be worth salvaging. Joe and I rassled it ashore on a low tide, caulked it and painted it, and it served us for many years.

When construction began on the Chesapeake Bay Bridge in the late 1940s, Olin joined the surge of builders who flocked to the site to find work. He moved his family into a roomy house about half a mile down the road from us.

Olin's problem with drink haunted him all his life. He lost his driver's license, owned no car, and always visited us on foot. His teeth were all gone, except for one lone survivor in the very front but he had no hesitation tackling an apple. As a craftsman, a man who worked with wood, he belonged neither to those described as watermen who made their living crabbing, fishing and tonging for oysters, or to a class -- which held themselves a cut above the watermen -- landowners who farmed.

Olin's wife Mabel was a woman of no discernable charm. She would, however, reach fearlessly into a bushel basket of live crabs and snatch out the largest. She would kill a grasshopper between her thumb and forefinger. No nonsense, this woman, one who had lived a life of hardship, had given birth to children only to see them die; had lived with a husband who drank hard. Mabel had pumped every drop of water she had ever used, winter and summer, year in and year out, her whole life through.

# # #

Mabel had a sister named Anita, married to David Sears whose stepfather was Olin's brother. This tangled web was commonplace on the isolation of the Eastern Shore. When he was a child David and his brother and sister had lived in the house with his mother and stepfather. David's mother had come down to Taylor's Island from her Baltimore home to escape the summer heat of their row house. She and the children had boarded the *Emma Giles* in Baltimore early in the morning, Mrs. Sears holding the younger children tightly by the hand as they made their way up the gangplank.

David never mentioned where they had stayed but taking in summer boarders was a source of cash income on the Island where money was scarce. It was on such a summer trip that David's mother met Olin's brother, fell in love, divorced Mr. Sears and married Mr. Horseman. And moved into this house that seemed fated to draw lovers through its welcoming doors.

David, who had lived in the house as a boy, liked to tell how cold it was in the bedroom when he woke up on a winter's morning. He would throw on his clothes, hurl himself down the steep flight of steps and seek the warmth of the kitchen where his stepfather had fired up the woodstove, coffee was boiling and his mother was cooking breakfast.

David did his lessons at the kitchen table by the light of an oil lamp. If his mother asked him to get some water, he ran out to the well about 50 yards from the house.

###

Joe and Anita Lambden followed David's parents as tenants in the house. Joe was a self-confessed womanizer, who once, in the brick Methodist Church, in front of a Sunday school class, told the assembled youngsters and adults that he could no more see a woman walk by without lusting after her than turn down cold water on a hot day.

David and Anita met while they were both working at the Harrington Cannery and fell passionately in love. As David once told me, they couldn't keep their hands off each other.

One day, after a close call, David realized he'd have to leave the Island. "If Joe Lambden ever catches us, he'll kill us both," he told Anita.

The United States had entered World War II and David joined the Army   where he trained to be a cook. He was a man of slight build but strong and sinewey -- a build typical of many men of the area. A high-pitched voice seemed to go with the physique. He smoked quantities of unfiltered Camel cigarettes and was endlessly accommodating.

While he was in the Army, wherever he went, he kept in touch with Anita, sending the letters to his mother, who passed them along.

In time, Joe Lambden was persuaded to give Anita a divorce. She and David were married and lived happily ever after on Taylor's Island.

The garden Anita kept in front of their house was to be envied. Early every morning, wearing a sunbonnet, she was out hoeing the flawless rows of beans and tomatoes she had planted. Any upstart weed was instantly banished. Anita kept to herself; I never saw her socializing with the other women on the Island. Divorce was still frowned on.

# # #

In time, a Philadelphian named Ignatius Loyola Byrne, a printer at a newspaper there, bought the house. The earliest outsiders to come down to the Eastern Shore came from Philadelphia. Their drive, while a long one, did not entail crossing the Chesapeake Bay by ferry, as Baltimoreans and Washingtonians had had to do. Our next-door neighbors, Lee and Ann Jones, were Philadelphians.

Mr. Byrne and his family used the house as a summer refuge. In partnership with Staplefort Neild, he kept a small herd of cattle on the land behind the house. Byrne's decision to sell was half-hearted. Our real estate agent explained how he waffled and seesawed. First he wanted one price, and then when an offer came in, he asked twice as much. The realtor, driven to desperation by this equivocating, told him when we made our offer, to take it. Otherwise, he'd be hard-pressed to find another agent who would put up with his shenanigans.

Byrne, too, left behind a legacy: he had been conned by a Philadelphia contractor into having the house sprayed from top to bottom with a putty-like substance "guaranteed" to caulk up every possible chink through which water might find its way during a downpour. The window frames, the doors, their lintels, their framework, and the clapboard siding were encased in a rock-hard, grey coating that resisted all efforts to remove it. Guarantee aside, this coating proved ineffectual against the mysterious points of entry a heavy rain could discover when no carpenter could. It gave nothing but an ugly look to a house that deserved better.

# # #

When we bought the house we lived in Washington, D. C. We had   recently returned from Yugoslavia where Joe had served as Press   Attaché and Public Affairs Officer at the American Embassy in Belgrade. Our Island neighbors never managed to quite piece together what Joe did. It didn't seem to particularly interest them. They concluded he was some kind of foreign correspondent, and we left them with that simple explanation of our comings and goings.

Distance

Although we had had to settle for a three-hour drive to find a house on the water that we could afford, we set off on Friday nights like lovers bound for a tryst, heading for the Island -- Joe at the wheel, I beside him and Mary in the back with dolls and toys to while away the time.

Through Annapolis, across the Bay Bridge, down Route 50, not making a great deal of time on a road network that was awaiting improvement and expansion, sometimes slowed to a crawl behind a cantaloupe truck, across the Choptank River, and, at last, turning west on Route 16, we made our way to the Slaughter Creek bridge.   The planks on its deck set up a clatter, awakening Mary, who christened it   "The Bumpety Bridge."

We still had five miles to go along Taylor's Island's dark, narrow roads   past Grace Church, white and ghostly on the right, past the Brick Church and its shadowy graveyard, past houses, now at 11 o'clock silent and dark, until, finally we reached the lane leading to our own house, and our reward for hours on the road -- that musky, welcoming smell when we opened the kitchen door.

Although we were no more than 50 miles from Washington as the crow flies, we had entered another world. In the night sky the stars crowded each other for elbow room. Except for the whisper of the water, there was no sound.   Until, off in the loblolly pines, the hoot of an owl reminded us it was time for bed.

There were other reminders of our remoteness: the matter of a telephone, for instance.   It hadn't entered our minds when we took the house to ask about telephone service.   We should have.   Lee Jones, our next door neighbor on Taylor's Island, called me in Washington and introduced himself.   We had not yet met, but might he ask if we planned to have telephone service?   What a strange question, I thought.   We had taken telephones for granted wherever we had lived in Eastern Europe, in the Balkans.   And now, here in the United States, my neighbor wants to know if I plan to have one? How's that for culture shock?

He explained. There was no telephone line down the road that led to both our houses. When he wanted to make a phone call he had to drive up to his daughter's house, a mile or so distant, and use her phone. And if that pesky road was a morass -- well, no road, no phone.

Lacking an official name "that pesky road" was called Pine Top. It still is. It had been cut through by a lumber company timbering out loblolly pine trees for paper pulp. Tree trunks had been laid over the original track as paving and they were later covered with a thick layer of sandy soil, resulting in a washboard surface. The lumbermen moved on when they were finished, unconcerned about the upkeep or reliability of the road

And the telephone company, Lee explained, wanted an arm and a leg to run a line along this track to the Jones home. Enter the Kolareks. It was easy to tell from the tenor of our conversation that Lee Jones had his fingers crossed and was hoping we would spring for a share in the expense of laying a phone line. I thought a minute or two and said, yes, let's go ahead. Life without a phone when there is a small child in the family seemed unwise.

And so, before they had ever met, the Joneses and Kolareks shared a party line in addition to a stretch of undependable road.

Ann and Lee Jones, with two school-age daughters, had been among the first outsiders to make their way down to Taylor's Island from Philadelphia. Lee -- everybody called him Jonesy -- described his first trip to the island like this:

"It was a dry July day in 1949 when we first came down to look at the property and decided to buy. We had made good time from our home in Philly to Cambridge -- only five hours. The ride out to the property was a long half-hour, and the dusty surface of the Piney Peril (Jonsey's own name) gave us landlubbers no hint of its capacity for trouble.

"We bought the place on the spot," he said. "We never gave a moment's thought to mosquitoes, snakes, high water, the difficulties of transporting building materials and the capacity of the Piney Peril for betrayal and cussedness."

"And," he continued, "we began to formulate plans that stretched far into the future. The temporary shelter we had put up for starters was transformed in our dreams into an attractive rambler with a picture window looking out over the creek. The flat-bottomed rowboat our two little girls paddled around in, grew in imagination to a graceful boat with gay canopies where we and our friends sipped long, cooling drinks and the fish devoured our bait and leaped to the decks, pleading for more."

The Jones' dream was, in time realized, and they moved into a comfortable split-level house they had built, with a picture window giving a view over the water. A luxuriant mimosa tree flourished out front. But it was two years before they were able to get telephone service.

Jonesy had many stories about his battles with the Piney Peril. My favorite is the one about the night, after a long, wet drive down from Philadelphia, his rear wheels found their home in a deep rut and would not budge. Leaving Ann in the car, he walked more than a mile in a driving rain, got the one-seat tractor out of the garage, hooked it up to a flatbed trailer, put a chair on the trailer, grabbed an umbrella and conducted his wife home like Cleopatra on a Nile barge.

Our family enjoyed one summer in the house before Joe was assigned to a post in Africa. We stayed two years in Conakry, Guinea, while our daughter turned from a three-year old child into a schoolgirl. The economic situation in that country was so bleak we rated additional "hardship pay." And, since there were absolutely no commodities to be had there, we came home with plans about spending the surplus that we had accumulated.

Our first trip back to the house after a two-year absence brought a great surprise. The Piney Peril had been covered with black top! We celebrated appropriately with Ann and Lee Jones. "First a telephone, then a hardtop road," Jonesy said, raising his glass: "Our cup runneth over!"

Not Just Distant -- Invisible

We kept discovering the delights of remoteness. Take privacy. No one could see our house, we could see no others. Our nearest neighbors, the Joneses, were at least a mile away. Across the creek we could make out the silhouettes of a couple of places. For a woman who had always lived in cities where window shades were as essential as running water, this was heady stuff. Returning to the simple joys of childhood, I ran naked in a pelting rain, the drops stinging my skin. I felt invisible.

And I came to realize that invisibility was endemic to the area. Nobody had ever heard of Taylor's Island. Indeed, one historian called the people who settled the Chesapeake Bay area "invisible people . . . petty planters who lived in one-room houses, raised tiny crops and never read a book . . ."[9] Detail about these early folk are as hard to pick out of history books as meat out of black walnuts shells.

Taylor's Island persisted in keeping a low profile. Nobody outside that vast expanse of wetlands that makes up Dorchester County, had ever heard of the place. Other islands have gained fame, some for their isolation some for their accessibility. Taylor's Island remains unseen, unnoticed.

President Clinton once spent a day there duck hunting. Photographs taken with Island notables appeared on the front pages of newspapers all over the country. The following day when I mentioned that we had lived on Taylor's Island for many years I heard, "*What Island?* What are you talking about?"

Not long after that, Peter Jennings, ABC's star anchorman, featured a long interview with an Island hero on his Person in the News feature. Milton Shenton, famous for being the first American GI to enter Paris following its liberation in World War II, told all about it.[10] [11] And Mr. Jennings explained that

---

[9] *Maryland: A History 1632 – 1974.* Edited by Richard Walsh and William Lloyd Fox. Maryland Historical Society, Baltimore, Maryland 1974. P. 44.

[11] See page 61.

Milton came from Taylor's Island.   Who remembers?
Nobody!

Here some 400 people put up with isolation and
mosquitoes -- but enjoy all the crabs and oysters they can eat
and a plentiful supply of corn on the cob in season, wonderfully
tasty tomatoes -- best in the world -- and cantaloupe you just
can't beat--sweet, juicy, full of flavor.

Slaughter Creek has broads and narrows, places where the
creek runs slow and shallow and places where the channel is
narrow and deep. I once suggested that we rename the Taylor's
Island Homemakers   the Slaughter Creek Broads, but found no
support.

And where it protrudes into the Chesapeake Bay, Taylor's
Island creates the narrowest point on the Bay and talk of
building a bridge connecting the western shore with the island
rises and falls like the tide. Nothing happens, perhaps because
the most prevalent bumper sticker in the area read: "THERE IS
NO LIFE WEST OF THE CHESAPEAKE BAY."

American patriotic literature celebrates "purple mountain's
majesty" and "the hills of home." Flat places go unsung. The
island is totally flat, much is marshland, and loblolly pines
abound.

Across Slaughter Creek from us there was a property called
"Poverty Point." Joe and I were instantly taken by the name.
It seemed apt. It had alliteration and rhythm. We envied it.
And we tried to come up with a name to describe our own
place. We had plenty of colorful models.

There was "Mulberry Grove."   "Taylor's Folly."
"Armstrong's Hogpen." "Neighbor's Neglect." "Homny Pot. "
But we were never able to come up with a name that was
exactly right. It was just "The House," anonymous and unsung,
like Taylor's Island, itself.

Mulberry Madness

The four mulberry trees on the western side of the house caused us some concern.   We felt pretty sure they were ancient; their branches spread wide and they provided welcome shade when the summer sun burned hot in the afternoon. When we bought the place two rotting tree trunks lay on the ground, helter-skelter, where they had fallen, a reminder that trees do blow down.   And the prevailing winds came from the west.   Any one of those trees could blow over and seriously damage the house.   If that should happen while we were absent, no one was available to intervene.

How these mulberry trees came to be there is an interesting story.

The oldest house on Taylor's Island lay on Oyster Cove and was called Mulberry Grove.   The Augustine Herrman map shows "Oester cove" and indicates a "plantation" on its banks. Originally named Dover, the house was said to date back to the 1660s.

It was on the market in 1960 when we were house hunting and we stopped to look at it. There were over 20 acres going for $22,000.   Its owner, James Spicer -- the same James Spicer with the Mogul tractor for whom young Bill Keene had worked -- had recently died at an advanced age and his many heirs wanted to get rid of the place.

The long lane that led up to the house was lined with dilapidated out- buildings crying for instant repair.   Inside, the old section of the house could claim a handsome staircase and little else.   Without extensive updating, it was hardly livable. There was no inside plumbing; a pump outside the kitchen provided water. The single obligatory light bulb dangled from the kitchen ceiling.

The name Mulberry Grove derived from a nineteenth century effort to establish a silk industry on the Eastern Shore. For centuries China managed to control the secret of her silk industry, until, one spinner of yarns related, a member of the

Pattison family, owner of Dover, at the risk of life and limb, smuggled out cocoons and mulberry seed, hoping to set up a silk industry on the Eastern Shore. But a good legend is easier to spin than fine silk.[12]

It's not hard to understand why the idea appeared to have merit. Summers were hot and, Lord knows, insects abounded. Why not silk worms, given a hearty diet of mulberry leaves? There was a demand for the product. At the time Dover was built, Louis XIV was holding sway in France, his court jam packed with men in silk stockings and women in bouffant silk dresses.

The best account I have found of the endeavor is contained in Elliott Buse's little book, *150 Years of Banking on the Eastern Shore.* He calls it the "Great Morus Multicaulis Mania," after the Latin name of the mulberry tree grown in the region. I call it "Mulberry Madness." Mulberry trees sprang up everywhere, Mr. Buse says. "Apparently this new 'mania' was germinating as early as 1826," and adds (you can almost see him smile): "A little later it really blossomed." Why not? In Paterson, N. J., a silk mill had been established as early as 1820.

Mr. Buse continues: "Farmers who had trees sold 'buds' at high prices and these produced 'switches' from which more 'buds' were sold." It sounds like a sort of pyramid scheme. And like many of them, it fizzled.

Unwinding the thread from the fragile cocoons proved difficult. One source speculated that farm wives, accustomed to all kinds of hard work, from scooping the meat out of tortoise shells to tending a flax patch, did not have the delicate touch this fine work demanded.

There is no evidence that the area ever produced any appreciable amount of silk, although prizes were announced at fairs for sewing silk and silk stockings. One fair offered a pistole for the best pair of stockings.

No doubt our stand of mulberry trees was the result of Mulberry Madness. We decided they would have to go. Some

---

[12] Encyclopedias say that a couple of Persian monks smuggled cocoons and mulberry seed in hollow bamboo canes out of China. And there was a well-established silk industry in France.

gentlemen of color living on the Island volunteered to do the job in exchange for the wood. It was a deal.   In one of the trees they discovered a bees' nest heavy with honey. The flight from the bumblebees added merriment for most, anguish for a few.   One of the men said that he had heard that banging on pots and pans would cause bees to swarm and leave.   We tried it, enthusiastically, 3-year-old Mary in the vanguard, to no avail.

Within a couple of days nothing was left but four massive tree stumps.   So much for Mulberry Madness.

Mulberry Grove after its restoration.

"Cator's Ancient Duplex"

The Cator House, another venerable building on the Island, was gone by the time we arrived. The Cator family -- of which William, Captain of the Billow and his son Tom of the missing ring, were members -- had left the Island by the beginning of the 20th century. Miss Emily, Tom's daughter, who had been born in Cambridge, was the last remaining member bearing the Cator name. She came to the Taylor's Island Homemakers Club with Laura Robinson Navy in Laura's old car, as undependable as it was large. They often missed a meeting.

Emily Cator was a doll-like woman of charm and humor. Although she must have been a beautiful girl, she had never married, having been born with a withered arm. Such an impediment in her day might very well have kept her out of the social whirl. She held a job of some importance at the Court House, and enjoyed a status appropriate to the venerable name she bore. She subscribed to a Philadelphia newspaper and read *Antiques* magazine.

However, this demure, lady-like package held a big surprise. Miss Emily was a dedicated gambler. A bus trip to Atlantic City found her aboard. She took advantage of every opportunity. The Homemakers were celebrating Christmas at the Elks Club one year, and when the Whiskey Sours were gone and it was time to go in to dinner, Miss Emily could not be found -- until somebody peeped into the room where the Elks kept the one-arm bandits, which non-profit social clubs were permitted to operate.

On one of her trips to Atlantic City Emily fell and broke an arm. A few years later, returning from Las Vegas, she suffered a fall resulting in a more serious injury and retired from travel. Soon she gathered her most treasured antiques and moved into a Cambridge retirement home   where Joe and I visited her in the 1980s shortly before she died.

The Cator House in Cambridge was purchased by some new arrivals to the community, outsiders who had tired of Maryland fried chicken and crab cakes and wanted access to fine wines and veal piccata. They invested heavily in the establishment of a restaurant that reflected their tastes. The restaurant failed. Others tried to make a go of it. One owner opened "Miss Emily's Room" which became a popular watering hole. I expect Emily would have approved.

The other Cator House, the one on Taylor's Island, drew the attention of architectural historian Henry Chandlee Forman who managed to catch up with it in the nick of time, arriving, he writes, just before the "small cottage complex" was torn completely to the ground.

The house is said to have been the residence of Colonel Moses L. LeCompte, he who gave the land for the original Methodist Church. The last occupant was Mollie Cator, an aunt of Senator George Radcliffe.

Foreman titles a chapter of his book[13] "Cator's Ancient Duplex" and dates one section of the house back to the late 1600s. "House II, probably constructed in the early or mid-18th century formed a separate dwelling which had been moved from another location and shoved up against. . House I." He describes a staircase in House II with steep risers over 9 inches high, its width a scant 20 -1/2 inches. "To go up these steps, a six-foot man . . . would have to turn his shoulders slightly to the side as he ascended. Some fat people would not make it."

Moving buildings is a long established custom on the Eastern Shore. Erosion often forces people to move a house back from the water's edge. Then too, you could double the size of your home by moving a second building along side and cutting a door through.

Several generations of the Edmondson family had lived on Cator Cove and   left behind   gravestones in a family plot. When Emily died, I was reminded of a verse from one of them which Mr. Forman quotes:
"Sister thou wust mild and lovely
Gentle as the summer breeze
Pleasant as the air of evening
Dearest sister thou hast left us
Here thy loss we deeply feel . . ."

---

[13] *Old Buildings, Gardens and Furniture in Tidewater Maryland*, Tidewater Publishers, Cambridge, Maryland 1967.

There is a reprise to the story of Cator's Ancient Duplex. Not far from the site of the original Cator house a Baltimore couple, Tom and Betty Burke, built a vacation home to which they eventually retired. A year or so after Tom died, Betty decided to move back to Baltimore. She put the house on the market and a real estate agent planted a For Sale sign out front. One day as Betty was weeding her flower garden, a station wagon rolled up and stopped. Its passengers wanted to see the house and one of the women, looking out over the water from the dining room window, asked: "Would you happen to know where Cator Cove is?"

"You're looking at it," Betty said.

It was a sale. The Dixon sisters, Caroline and Helen, descended from the original Cator family, bought the house. They may not bear the Cator name, but they have the right genes. The first thing they did was to move a large storage shed from one side of the property to the other.

This small cottage on Cator Cove was a summer refuge for Larry and Bobsey Franks. Its narrow winding staircase closely resembles the one Foreman describes in Cator's Ancient Duplex.

Stairs

Although Charles Wilson Peale is famous for seven portraits of George Washington, his most successful painting is an almost life size picture of his sons Titian and Raphaelle standing at the foot of a staircase. A triumph of *trompe l'oeil* it is said that Washington walked by it one day and raised his hat to the two young men, standing there so lifelike.

Peale was a native of the Eastern Shore and our staircase was exactly like his. The ships' carpenters who built these early houses knew how to use every square inch of available space. They curled the stairs leading to the upstairs bedroom around the chimney in a cunning fashion which left room for a sizable cupboard in the chimneybreast. Our builder, whoever he may have been, worked in two or three smaller cubbyholes besides.

Those stairs were perilous. Called winders, they were triangular -- wide at the outside and narrow on the inside. They were steep. Mary fell down them more than once. They had another drawback. You couldn't move anything bigger than a breadbox up or down them.

The central part of the house which Joe called the Great Room long before the Yuppies reinvented the term, had random width pine flooring, windows with twelve over eight lights, a simple mantle at the fireplace and those eye-appealing stairs curving upward. Hearsay dated it from about 1815. The 1670 Herrman map of Wingfield Point shows three houses on its Slaughter Creek side, one of which appoximates the location of the Staplefort house, and an 1877 map has the spot marked with the name T. Staplefort.

The back room was clearly an add-on with a small step down. It was narrower than the great room. An ugly staircase, a botched effort to imitate the curving one, competed for floor space with a monstrous kerosene space heater. Both had to go, and once we were rid of them the room became airy and inviting.

Unlike garrulous old people, old houses hold their secrets. Not until we removed the plaster and laths and exposed the skeleton of the rear section did we discover that its corner posts were simply young tree trunks, rather slender ones at that. Bare of bark, they had never been beveled square. They stood round and proud, still showing stumps where branches had been lobbed a long, long time ago.

The plaster was mixed with horsehair to help it stick together and was applied over rough-hewn laths. The studs were closer to each other than we place them today and were braced every so often with struts, again the work of carpenters accustomed to building ships. From this back room we installed a flight of steps that rose gently upward to the rear bedroom. At last we could move box springs and other pieces of furniture to the second floor. But I never lost the sense that the rear room depended on the strength of those four slender, young tree trunks and I consistently hesitated to overload them.

From this upstairs room a flight of steps as steep as a ladder took you to the attic. The attic was empty except for a black Bakelite horn that had once been part of an old Victrola, left behind by some previous tenant. Otherwise, it was bare; there was not even a chair. Bare boned and dusty, it offered no distractions. Here time stood still.

When we had come back home after years spent in the Balkans in a country torn apart by political strife, or returned from a part of Africa still living in a previous millennium, or from a divided Germany emerging from a destructive war and the Holocaust, its former capital split asunder by an ugly wall, it was then I liked to go up to the attic.

I would wait, wait for the normal routines of life to be reestablished; wait until the pulse moved at a steady beat. And when I was alone in the house I would climb up this last steep flight of steps. Sunshine oozed through the cracks between the shakes and fell in patches on the floor. The hand-hewn rafters had once oozed drops of resin, now hard as amber. It was very quiet in the attic. Bare boned and dusty, it offered no distractions.

Here the many whirling, eddying components of me, of my self, could come together like a great flock of black birds swirling through the air, looking for a field to light.

In our way of life, wandering from place to place, you cultivate a sense of disconnection with yesterday. You learn to leave the past behind; to say goodbye and not look back. And while you may enjoy the experience of moving from one strange place to another, adapting to foreign customs, limping along in a foreign language, you risk losing fragments of your identity. You suffer a lack of connection, of belonging, of permanence.

Up in this quiet old attic where time stood still, I was anchored. The attic accepted me, held me, and gave me a sense of permanence. It invited me to stay. I belonged.

Exactly ten years after we had bought the house, our traveling days came to an end with Joe's retirement from the Foreign Service. Now we could devote ourselves to turning this plain Jane of a house into an attractive, year-round home. Between our arrival in April of 1970 and the end of the school year, Mary attended seventh grade at the Cambridge Middle School. The bus picked her up before 8 a.m., and she got home after 4 p.m. It made for a very long day and left little time for after-school activities. Faced with winter, short days and bad road conditions, we were torn.

Then, too, retirement fitted Joe like a pair of too-tight shoes. He needed something to keep him active in his profession. We solved both problems by moving to Columbia, Md., the New American City, half way between Washington and Baltimore. Joe returned to his first love, newspaper editing, at the *Washington Post.* Mary entered a brand-new school where all the pupils were new kids on the block and remained there until she graduated in1975. I burnt up the road between Columbia and Taylor's Island, overseeing renovations at my beloved house.

And, in time, from a shabby weekend refuge at the end of a rutted lane, I transformed it into a handsome home of which anyone could be proud. When Mary went off to college, Joe and I moved in. It was now home. Our only home.

A real country kitchen.

100

The Woodstove

There was a woodstove in the kitchen when we bought the house; not one of those decorative cast iron wonders that need frequent applications of stove polish.   It was a no-nonsense white enamel stove with a thermometer set in the oven door.   It dated it back to the 1930s.   We were fortunate to have it when early spring and late fall brought a cold snap.   Joe was adept at building a fire, a skill he learned as a Scout.   His old Boy Scout Handbook ranked second only to his catechism.   He could fire that woodstove up before you could say "It's chilly in here."

Of all the appliances strewn about the kitchen -- a generous 14' by 14' -- it was the most attractive.   The sink, a relic with long, spindly legs, stood under the window with a westerly view over our field.   From the electric cook stove, in the far corner, I could look out over the water to the east.   But the refrigerator was 'way over against a third wall.   For storage, we used an ugly little metal stand painted the same sickly green as everything else in the kitchen.   Don't ask about counter space.   There was none.   I could walk a mile to fix a meal.   But for weekends and vacations it served.

I learned not to trip over the vinyl floor tiles that curled at the corners and to duck where the ceiling barely cleared the top of my head.   Above it was the spooky attic full of old mud dauber nests accessible via the scuttyhole upstairs.

I spent hours dreaming of the day when I would have a kitchen both beautiful and practical.   A dozen years went by before that miracle was achieved.   I was not around when the contractor knocked down the ceiling to reveal a high-pitched roof, called now a days by real estate agents "a cathedral ceiling."   And a few weeks later I walked in to see new shoulder-high paneling and cupboards fashioned out of weather-aged silvery siding from the old cowshed.   A carpenter called "Porky" Trice had done a beautiful job and I enjoyed a moment of breathtaking happiness.

From a wheel we had found among the remnants of a farm wagon buried in high weeds, a young neighbor had fashioned a handsome chandelier.   We moved our round dinner table and Windsor chairs in and sat down.   It was a far cry from the old,

101

scruffy kitchen with mismatched chairs, excelsior spilling from their seats.

The woodstove, however, was gone. We had installed central heating, which kept us warm on even the coldest days. We could now enjoy the house at Thanksgiving and Christmas, and looked toward a day when we could live there year 'round.

In a fit of pride and hospitality I invited David Sears to come by and see the transformation. Ever since we had bought the place, David had spent hours there patching and fixing. Over coffee we had heard dozens of stories about his childhood in the house -- how cold it could be in that upstairs bedroom on a winter's morning and how he grabbed his clothes and tore down those curving steps to the kitchen to dress in front of the woodstove.

On this first visit to the new kitchen David walked through the door and his face fell. It was no longer the familiar place he had known as a boy, the kitchen where his father had started a fire in the woodstove at first daylight, where he had run shivering to dress by its warmth, where his mother had cooked him a hot breakfast and sent him off to school. The room of a million memories was gone and I suspect he never forgave me for destroying the beloved old family kitchen he had once known.

But all he said was: "I see you got rid of the woodstove."

Mosquitoes

The lowly light bulb and Pandora's box had much in common. Both could, in an instant, let loose a flock of misfortunes. Turn on the light and every insect in that marshland known as Taylor's Island came flying, buzzing, pushing and finally, after biting, dying in windrows on the table tops, on the floor, in the corners. After a thorough house cleaning a warm buggy night was bound to follow. We quickly solved the mystery of the dark green ceiling in the great room. It was an effort to cut down on the insect invasion.

I had dreamed of weekends in the country, going to bed with a book and having an hour's read before falling asleep. The dream became a nightmare. The bed lamp invited mosquitoes and gnats to come in and sing to me in their thin whine and explore my ears, swarming without mercy around my head and neck. Slapping, flailing of arms were to no avail. I learned to turn the light off and fall asleep to the music of the spring peepers singing their mating songs or in autumn, to the sound of flocks Canada geese flying over.

When we got rid of the glaring fluorescent tube in the ceiling of the kitchen we could stir a pot on the stove without peppering the contents with tiny no-see-ums. And, in time, we caught on to the yellow-tinted light bulbs, and installed them. Their soft glow reminded me of Bobby Spicer's string of Christmas lights.

The Dorchester County mosquito has given rise to jokes like "Our mosquitoes are so big that they carry hostesses on board." Robert Shenton called the mosquito "our national bird." And one Sunday in the 1940s they were so thick that services at Grace Church had to be cancelled. The service record notes: "No church. Too many mosquitoes."

So what did we do? Well, we learned. We learned not to go out when the air was still. Innocents who imagined that the banks of Slaughter Creek were the equal of the wide beaches of Atlantic City and smeared their bodies with fragrant suntan oil and stretched out on a canvas beach chair to get a nice tan, were doing nothing more than yelling "Dinner. Come and get it!" to the female anopheles. Because, as I am sure you know, it's only the female of this species that flies about collecting samples of human blood.

Your worst enemy is a still day when the surface of the water is dead flat and there is not a breath of air. If, however, you have the gumption to take a dishtowel and wave it vigorously around your head and ears, with an occasional swipe at your calves, and wear pants and long-sleeved cotton shirts, you might get to the clothes line and back with no more than a dozen bites.

The mosquito's worst enemy is a stiff breeze. If you have an outdoor chore that can be put off, put it off until you look out and the trees are bending in the wind and whitecaps are forming on the water. Then you may be safe.

Over the years, as I was bothered less and less by attacks, I began to suspect that the breed had tired of my flavor and moved on to tastier expanses of flesh. Or maybe I had subconsciously adopted enough good habits and tricks to minimize attack.

Mosquito Control -- Manmade Version

Along about the time we arrived in the area, the Dorchester County Roads Board had instituted a program of mosquito control. That the name included the word "control" was a blunder. Mosquito *control* borders on false advertising. Nevertheless the Dorchester County Roads Board was stuck with it and was mandated to send trucks to regularly spray the insecticide malathion in infested areas. That meant all over Taylor's Island, among other low-lying areas of the county.

In order to keep the cost down, a factor when the program was new and on probation, Staplefort Neild had gone from household to household, explained this spraying business and collected the $5.00 annual fee for a visit once a week by the spray truck. He knew everybody, they knew him, and Lord knows, spraying for the pesky critters was worth a try. As a result, no bills had to be mailed and administrative expenses were kept in check. The Roads Board got a list of subscribers from Staplefort and the young men who drove the trucks knew where to spray.

Who could have foreseen the confusion, the misunderstanding, and the controversy as years passed and people unfamiliar with the history of the system forked over their $5 for a year's worth of mosquito control? My husband, who had volunteered to take a crack at the collecting as Staplefort's health declined, had all the patience of a man whose life had been governed by impending deadlines. I am certain he collected the fee from many people who had no idea what they were actually getting, or who was supplying it, but thought they were getting what was advertised: mosquito control.

One newcomer to the Island, driven wild by the swarms of mosquitoes assailing him toward dusk one calm summer's day, (mosquitoes can smell new blood from miles away) called Joe on the telephone and spent some time explaining to him how he ought to get out of the business of mosquito control if he couldn't deliver what he promised. He did not pause long enough to hear that he was speaking to a hapless volunteer whose involvement with the program was marginal, and when this fact was borne in on him, he never fully recovered from his embarrassment.

Joe, disgusted after calls from dissatisfied customers who were not getting their $5-worth of mosquito control, telephoned the roads board to say he quit. "Oh, no!" the young woman in the office admonished. "You can't quit until you find somebody to take your place." Remember that oarsman on the river Styx?

How Mother Nature Handles Mosquitoes

The praying mantis is so birdlike we had trouble thinking of ours as an insect. Ours -- the one Mary and I found in residence on our screen porch -- was green, had enormous eyes, and was ample-jawed and prayerful. Mary named her Genevieve. We hadn't expected her to stick around, but she seemed at home there and weekend after weekend we caught her perched on the back of a wicker chair or scrambling up the screening.   She could easily have left by way of a crack between the floorboards, but she seemed to find our supply of bugs ample and our wicker furniture comfortable. In the early years the wealth of insect life that made its way through the breaks in the screen or up through the spaces between the old floorboards gave her an ample diet. She moulted twice, each time leaving a delicate carapace clinging to the screen from tiny claws. Each time she emerged more lustrous, sleeker.

We kept an eye out before we plumped down on the porch cushions.   We didn't want to mash Genevieve as we had sometimes mashed the little lizards that had roamed our house in Africa. We needn't have worried. Genevieve took excellent care of herself.   And we certainly enjoyed watching her feast on some morsel that might otherwise have feasted on us.

As autumn approached we wondered how Genevieve would find a mate and deposit her distinctive egg sac to hatch out next spring.   Again, we needn't have worried.   She managed quite well, because the following spring Genevieve Two took up residence.

Every spring brought a new Genevieve and we lost count. We always welcomed the sight of mantis egg sacs on foliage. While others ordered them from nursery catalogs, ours came free and abundant.

After Olin Horseman rebuilt the porch for us and put plywood on the floor, we thought we had seen the end of Genevieves. But no, the next spring, there she was, No. VIII perched on the back of a chair. One autumn afternoon I noticed a large brownish male on the   screen outside. Genevieve was on the inside of the screen, and the two insects were approaching each other, slowly, slowly.   I went out to the kitchen and gave them some privacy.

The female praying mantis is said to eat her mate after they have coupled, not an act of cannibalism, but because she needs his hormones in order for their offspring to develop. She then leaves her egg sac under a leaf, or on a twig and goes off to die, herself.

A *New Yorker* cartoon recently showed a hangdog praying mantis returning home to his spouse. He is headless. "You slept with her, didn't you?" the caption reads.

Spiders

Spider webs. Perfectly formed, a dewdrop glistening on their silk -- they have the beauty of mathematics. The spiders were a busy lot around our house, inside and out. In the early years of dilapidation, I encouraged them to take up residence inside. Outside they needed no invitation. I never killed a spider. We bade them welcome and offered a cuisine of variety and abundance.

Early in the morning, on the kitchen porch, great miracles of weaving would appear, created overnight. Vectors of support strung almost haphazardly, held concentric octagons, nonagons, pentagons, and in the center, the spider extending her invitation to step into her parlor. I have stared hypnotized with wonder at the tiny, vulnerable creators of these architectural wonders dozing in the center, as day light cut off their supply of prey.

Purple Martins

Everybody on the Eastern Shore passionately woos purple martins, those gregarious swallows that choose to live in lofty apartments provided for them by people who like what they do. What they do is consume incredible numbers of mosquitoes.

People buy specially built bird condominiums and mount them on high poles in the hope that martins will choose to nest in them.

These handsome birds are called purple martins because their feathers are a shiny dark bluish-purple. Their folded wings come to a sharp point giving them a distinctive profile. And they dart and soar in the early evening when mosquitoes become active and are a pleasure to watch as they gorge themselves.

I never succeeded in attracting martins to the second-hand birdhouse a friend gave me. We mounted it high on a pole at

107

the water's edge and watched and waited. A pair of birds, accompanied by a third, came to inspect the house one morning. The couple flew around it, hovering over it, twittering as my heart fluttered with hope.

"What do you think?" the wife asked.

"Well," said the husband, "I smell cat around here." The third bird, clearly a real estate agent, reluctantly admitted that a number of feral cats lived in a nearby barn.

"Let's look a little further," the wife suggested, and the three flew away.

Soon another couple, with real estate agent, appeared, hovered and twittered.

"It's not exactly brand new, but the porch is nice and wide," the wife said.

"Porch, smorch," snorted the husband. "Look at those big holes. Sparrows can crowd right in, and you know what that means. Bye bye birdie."

"You're right," said the wife and off they flew, agent in tow.

And so it went, couple after couple came to look and reject. It was no sale for the agent and a summer without martins for me.

Aside from their enormous appetite for mosquitoes, martins are fun to watch. Five, six or more families often move into a well-constructed martin house, much as city folk crowd into condominiums. People relate to them, watch their comings and goings and keep a protective eye as they fledge their young. One devoted bird watcher once explained to me that the mother bird actually housebreaks the babies.

I should have bought one of Howard Richardson's bird houses and shrugged at the cost. Howard was the Frank Lloyd Wright of martin houses. His store, in Church Creek at the crossroads of Route 16 and the Blackwater Refuge road, was a favorite stopping off place for Joe after a long day's fishing. Mr. Richardson served up an orange drink at his soda fountain that was irresistible. He kept the formula secret. Also secret was the source of the half-dozen chairs that lined his fountain. Their design exactly matched molded plastic chairs of today but they were carved from wood. And like all proper soda fountain chairs, they swiveled.

But his *pieces de resistances*   were the martin houses he built.   He displayed them outside his store, right where the crossroads traffic couldn't miss them.   And even in this busy spot, martins often moved right in.   You could buy a house already tenanted.   Why didn't I do that?

Mr. Richardson's martin houses were as richly populated as the one in this sketch by Eric Dennard.

Cap'n Robert Shenton's Store

Miss Ida minds the store while Cap'n Robert fillls my gas tank.

David Sears stops to chat.

The Country Store

Sam Jones's General Store, where the Church Creek Fire Company now stands, was such an unholy mess, so dilapidated and so attractive in the way an auto wreck is attractive, that newspapers as far away as the *Baltimore Sun* wrote an occasional feature about it. The *Sun* rated it the worst kept store in Maryland.

It was gone by the time we arrived, but its memory lingered on. Legend said that the cat slept atop the wheel of cheese to keep the rats away. Attributed to Maurice Rimpo, who was editor of the *Cambridge Banner*, is the story that "somebody came in to buy a piano, but Sam Jones couldn't find it."

The country store may be on its way out, but two still lingered on Taylor's Island for our enjoyment.

Robert Shenton's was one. Robert and his wife Ida ran the little store next door to the school house. Built around 1924, this school had already shut down in 1960 when we arrived on Taylor's Island and children were bussed to larger schools in outlying communities. Vacant and unused, it stood two-stories high, the four rooms on each floor lighted by large windows.

During the time it "kept" the school children had depended on Robert's store for candy and cookies, like the enormous ginger cookies -- they must have been two inches across -- that he kept in a glass jar on top of his display case, just out of reach of tiny tots. The cookies had a strong spicy flavor and you just reached in and took out as many as you wanted at a penny a-piece. When our nieces and nephews from Baltimore came to visit, a stop at Cap'n Robert's store for some of those cookies was a must. Then we came back from an absence of a few years to find the jar gone. The Health Department had raised a fuss about people reaching in and helping themselves, Robert told me.

He also dispensed bulk ice cream that Joe favored. He could buy half a pint, which was about as much as he would eat at a sitting, and bring it home in one of those little folding pasteboard containers with a metal bail like Chinese carry-out comes in. Robert would come into the store from out back where he might have been shucking oysters -- he sold them by the gallon jar -- or filling his kerosene tank, and he'd scoop out the ice cream with no time out for hand washing. I expect the Health Department people would have fallen over in a dead faint, but we never suffered any ill effects.

It would be wrong to call the store a gathering spot for the Island's non-drinkers. One chair and three square feet of floor space don't permit much gathering. But it was a refuge on a windy day with the little stove fired up, and you could plunk down in the only chair, nurse a soda for an hour and read the funny cards pinned on the walls.

The entire store was hardly more than 12 feet by 12 feet and every inch of the walls not occupied by shelves was covered by raunchy postcards and funny sayings. They had been supplied by friends who wandered further afield than Robert ever did. Some were postcards sent in the mail; some were unsuitable for mailing.

A sample of Robert's preference in humor went like this:

"How do I want to die? I want to be shot to death when I am 100 years old by a jealous husband who catches me in bed with his wife." Or: "Money cheerfully refunded to anyone accompanied by both parents who is over the age of 90." The words "who is over the age of 90" were printed in such small type they were virtually indecipherable.

Robert had been born in 1900 and could look back over a long, active life. He once told Joe he had worked on the water for fifty years, using the same boat, the 36-foot long Tiger with a 10 horsepower Briggs & Stratton engine.

His father, he said, used a 20-foot boat with one sail, but Robert stopped using sail around 1920. Back then "you got ten cents a bushel for crabs." In 1971, when he and Joe talked, he thought crabs were just as plentiful as ever.

"Crabs run in cycles. I don't see no difference. I've crabbed for a quarter of a cent a pound -- must be 40 pounds to a bushel," he said. The lowest price that crabs went for in 1970 was 6 cents a pound. Robert also swore by the oysters. "I think we got better and larger oysters" -- he, like all Islanders, said "ersters" -- "than we did years ago." He felt the state transplanting program was responsible and the 30-cent-a-bushel tax to pay for the program was worthwhile.

Tonging for oysters? "Well, after you get used it you don't mind it."

Making a living on the water is easier now than when he first started, Robert said, because you have rubber gloves, insulated boots and rubber rainwear.

He was not a tall man, but he was hard as nails. He once told Joe that when he could no longer get out on the water every day in *The Tiger* and crab or tong for oysters he'd be ready to die. His family gave him a big 90th birthday party in the Fire House. By then he was crippled by arthritis and when he died he hadn't been out on his boat for a while. But he had enjoyed a romance with an Island widow and given the gossips something to whisper about.

The country store to reckon with, however, stood on the right as you drove onto the Island. Once a part of the Harrington cannery, the store held more space than merchandise. A wooden bench about 10 feet long provided a social center when rain and cold drove people in off the porch. Watermen waited for "buy" boats to come along and purchase their day's catch, or hung out in the store if the weather was too bad to work. I expect their gossip was rare and juicy. I noticed that the minute I walked through the door they clammed up.

When we first arrived, back in 1960, a big muscular man with a hearty manner named Sol Bramble ran the store. He always stopped whatever he was doing to give Mary a piece of candy from a long row of glass jars full of the kind of penny candy Joe and I had known as kids. We thought it was extinct; it was only endangered.

Everybody liked Sol, especially the watermen. He opened at 5 a. m. to accommodate them when they needed to buy bull lips to use as crab bait.

Counters -- broad, 3-foot wide wooden counters -- lined the left wall of the store. On the opposite side, the Post Office took up most of the space.

Then we came home from an absence to discover the store in the hands of a curmudgeon named Grimes who just didn't like people. He was rude to his customers and downright abusive to Mr. Mace, the postmaster. That he should draw a regular paycheck from the Federal government infuriated Grimes, whose business dwindled as people grew tired of his surly manner. If you tried to help yourself and line up your purchases on the counter, he would snarl that this was not a self-service store. But he rose reluctantly to wait on you.

Finally the postmaster could no longer tolerate this poisonous atmosphere and moved lock, stock and boxes to a small building our one-armed carpenter, Albert Stanley, built at a nearby crossroads.

Grimes threw in the towel and was followed by George Harrison, his wife Annabelle and her mother, Jenny Wheatley. George had had some experience in the Cambridge A&P Store. Nobody ever just said "A&P." It was always the A&P Store.

The long bench down the middle of the big room still served as a social center. George had an off-premises license to sell beer. Although this forbade consumption inside the store, Bernard Horseman, one of Olin's brothers, followed the time-honored custom of keeping his opened quart bottle in a brown paper bag and sneaking a circumspect sip from time to time.

With the post office gone, Annabelle wanted to use the extra space to display handcrafted items   -- quilts, baskets, antiques, anything anybody wanted to sell including hand-painted oyster shells.   One day a blue and white chamber pot caught my eye. I picked it up and carried it over to the counter. Miss Jenny appeared from nowhere -- she was a tiny wren of a woman -- saw the pot sitting on the counter in plain view, turned bright red, nudged her daughter, and said, "Get that thing out of sight, Annabelle. It ain't fittin'." I took the chamber pot home and planted geraniums in it before I discovered it leaked. Caveat emptor.

Cancer and heart attacks carried Annabelle and George away, and Jenny succumbed to Alzheimer's.

Then a gale in the form of Erlyne Twining blew through the old building.

Take the word en - tre- pren - eur and wrap its syllables around Erlyne's waist and you have a perfect fit. She came along at a time when the store had gone out of business, shelves bare. All that fine empty space drew Erlyne like beer draws a drunk and she soon had the place jumping. First, a sit down bar. George Harrison had already upgraded the license for on-premises consumption. Then crab soup. Erlyne made the best cream of crab soup in the world. A generous sprinkle of tarragon atop each serving gave it a haunting exotic flavor that was addictive.

Her classic Maryland crab soup -- a hearty vegetable beef soup reinforced with chunks of crab, shell and all -- was four-star, too. She served her steaming bowls of soup, crab cakes and standards like ham and cheese and baloney sandwiches. Soon she could hardly keep up with the demand.

She put booths in the back and christened the place the Slaughter Creek Pub. The decor took on the random look of a yard sale. Erlyne cut a swathe through any kind of flea market: "I'll take that Bull Durham sign, and that -- no, the other over on the left -- yeah, and the old Coca Cola sign, and how about that sign from the railroad depot? Whatcha want for it?" They all found a place in the Pub.

Business boomed. The long bench down the middle gave way to a coffee buffet and racks of snack food. It was hard to tell what we had now. Country store? Yes. Pub? That, too.

Then it got to be the custom for Thom Garner, then Rector of Old Trinity Church in Church Creek and something of a gourmet, to gather up a handful of parishioners after Sunday services and drive down to the Pub for lunch. Erlyne's establishment was edging slowly, slowly upscale. The country store was crowding the country club.

Crabs and oysters were available from local watermen
who sold their wares at the landing behind the store.

Grace Church –Part Two

On the other hand, things were going downhill at Grace Church. The walnut pews were rarely full. After one service in the 1930s, a disconsolate minister wrote in the Jacobs Service Record Book: "Only three in attendance. Extremely discouraging."

It is hard to guess how the triumvirate who built the church envisioned Taylor's Island's future and harder yet to pinpoint why their high hopes turned to dust. Did they believe they were standing on the brink of skyrocketing, post-Civil War prosperity? It is hard to pinpoint why such high hopes turned to dist. Some of the old families had moved away, and who could blame them when you could live in Cambridge and enjoy modern comforts? Some of the old homes had burned to the ground. Steamships having replaced sail, shipbuilding no longer flourished. The Island's economy had not lived up to expectations.

Between 1924 and 1961 -- the period covered by the Service Record that turned up in a church closet -- notations by many ministers paint a sorry picture of a church in decline. Mother Nature was not helpful, either. In March 1942 a snowstorm on Palm Sunday prevented services from being held. Other mishaps: The bridge broke down -- no church; heavy rain -- service canceled; in January 1959 a deeply unhappy priest wrote "Very cold. No stove," his oversized "V" and "N" emphasizing the chill. And an undated entry: "No church. Too many mosquitoes." Finally, Thomas Bast, on March 7, 1947, after preaching to a flock of three, was understandably discouraged.

There was, however, a silver lining to these dark clouds in the person of Senator George Radcliffe. It was nothing short of miraculous the way he could draw a throng into Grace Church. In 1936 he was listed as preacher at a service when an alms basin given by Thomas H. Keene was dedicated in memory of Harry P. Spilman, and although all the Keenes and

Spilmans on the Eastern Shore were surely there, they hardly amounted to the total of 220 who attended.

Let's stop here and establish the Radcliffe connection with Taylor's Island. George M., the Senator's son, explains:

"My father's father was John Anthony LeCompte Radcliffe, whose family for generations has been associated in and around the Lloyds area [in the Neck District] . . . My grandfather's first wife was a Beckwith and after her death he married a widow whose maiden name was Sophia Delilah Travers. She was born on Taylor's Island and her Travers family had been there for generations . . ." How well we know.

It was a wish of Sophia Travers Radcliffe that her son "not only do something to assist Taylor's Island, but also to preserve Grace Church itself." Who better qualified than the man who had accompanied President Roosevelt on his yacht to the dedication of the Choptank River Bridge? Again, in 1939, the Senator overloaded the once-echoing building at a homecoming celebration when 280 were in attendance. Even with folding chairs crowding the aisle, it is hard to picture so many people jammed into the sanctuary.

Considering that the average attendance by 1939 had sunk to between 10 and 20, any sentient person had to conclude that George Radcliffe was a *non-pareil drawing* card. But it was not until 1950 that the Senator suggested the formation of the Grace Foundation of Taylor's Island. The idea took off. Its first annual report, signed by the Senator, himself, says that nearly 200 persons were present at the May 1951 meeting, "coming from as far away as Baltimore, Pennsylvania and Washington, D. C."

The group enthusiastically endorsed the acquisition and restoration of the old Chapel of Ease and it was soon moved to the grounds of Grace Church on the acre of adjoining land given by the Hudson Lumber Company with the "invaluable assistance of Mr. Byron Harrington" in facilitating this transaction.

A successful and long-lasting endeavor had been launched.

The public relations business lost a natural talent in George Radcliffe. He shone the spotlight of publicity on Taylor's Island time after time, bringing prominent Maryland figures down for ceremonies to commemorate historic events. In

1959, Maryland's Governor Tawes attended the installation of the historical marker in front of the church. You know about that.

Then, on the tenth anniversary of its placing, Cambridge newspapers carried pictures of the church, adding words about the Chapel of Ease. Yes, the Senator knew how to generate publicity. This led to a growing interest in the Foundation. Being a member became the thing to do. Members attended the Whitsunday service in May, stayed for a short meeting of the Foundation, had lunch on the church grounds, and drove around the Island looking for the site of a home place, or a grave marker. Many had been washed away.

In 1955, the Foundation membership visited the site of Old Trinity Church, where Colonel and Mrs. Edgar Garbisch were deeply involved in the restoration of the old building, dating back to around 1675. Mrs. Garbisch was heir to the Chrysler fortune and she and her husband had bought an estate not far from Old Trinity. They spared no expense in searching for a prototype in England, imported silversmiths, architects and other craftsmen. They personally played an active role in rebuilding the old church to resemble, as closely as possible, the original building. A dedicatory plaque reads: Old Trinity, circa 1675. This Episcopal Church was restored 1955-1960 as a memorial to Walter Percy Chrysler and his wife Ella Viola Forker by their daughter Bernice together with Edgar Wm Garbisch her husband."

In order to keep Grace Church viable, one service a month was held there from May to October, attended by the congregation of Old Trinity and conducted by her rector.

If Old Trinity Church had needed a face-lift, Grace Church on Taylor's Island was not far behind. Like women, as they age, wooden buildings require a great deal of maintenance to retain their grace and beauty   And, thanks to the Foundation, maintenance was forthcoming.

119

Raccoons had chewed holes in the shingles of the
steeple of Grace Church and bees had built honey-
heavy hives beneath the eaves over the side door.

The Ways of our Forefathers

Black snakes, they say, are voracious consumers of rats and mice. Given that premise, I expected the reptiles who wintered cozily in the double layer of soft pink insulation under our attic floorboards to reciprocate by devouring our rodents. But no. For years, every time we reopened the house in the spring, we found it infested with mice.

These were little white-footed field mice that came in out of the cold during the winter and I found their nests in bureau drawers and other unexpected spots, like the organ in Grace Church. I also noticed that every mouse nest contained a fragment of snake shed about the size of a large postage stamp. Would any naturalist like to explain this to me? My personal theory is that snakes shun their discarded sheds, and the fragment offers a sort of protection. I can see an advertisement in *Good Mousekeeping magazine*: "Snake Shed Fragments. Insurance against black snakes! Guaranteed. Order Now!"

Every winter, while nesting in the Grace Church organ, mice gnawed the insulation off its wires. One expert explained to me that the plastic insulation on those wires was derived from uric acid which is Mouse Martini. We had to get the organ fixed every year, until one spring the repairman came down, took one look, threw in the towel, and declared it beyond repair.

This sent me next door to the Chapel of Ease where an old-fashioned organ was stored in a corner, almost inaccessible behind broken chairs, boxes of who-knows-what and the other detritus that accumulates in seldom-used buildings. One Sunday after service in the church next door, our organist, an adventurous and vigorous young man, pushed and pulled his way though, sat down at the old organ, pumped the pedals vigorously and gave us a virtuoso concert.

Some years had gone by since then, and our organist of the year was a chubby woman of middle age who was disinclined to pump with the vigor of her young predecessor. Ever the problem solver, I found a gentleman who made his living converting old organs into electric-driven ones. For $238 he

121

electrified our relic, we moved it into the church, and it sounded a lot better than the electric organ had. One winter of depredation by mice had done more damage to our modern organ than years of neglect in an unheated building had done to the old reed organ. And a great many of its essential parts were made of leather.

Which leads me to compare the ways of our forefathers with our own and conclude that we do not always come out ahead.

Take the steeple on the church, which was dedicated in 1873. Raccoons were gnawing great holes in the shingles and something had to be done. But what? Contractors were cool to the idea of climbing its steep sides. Finally, a huge crane arrived from Salisbury and lifted the steeple off the church and set it aside, on the ground, to be repaired. Months later the crane returned and replaced the steeple. But somehow the cross at the top got left off.

Day in and day out I drove past this exercise and wondered every time how the original builders had managed to get that steeple up, apply shingles and top it with a cross, all without a crane from Salisbury. I cannot supply an answer. When the Bishop of the Diocese of Easton dedicated the church in 1873, he said the cost of construction had been $3,500. The crane from Salisbury alone may have run somewhere around that figure.

To understand why the Island wildlife claimed the building for their own you need to remember that services were held there only six times a year, from May to October, insuring that the church remained consecrated.

The area fauna, however, considered the building unoccupied and claimed it for their own. A flock of buzzards roosted, congregated, copulated and throve on the roof of the neighboring Chapel of Ease. I can assure you that a buzzard displaying his virile wingspan before a group of admiring lady buzzards is a sight not soon forgotten.

Raccoons, who are natively happy in penthouses, took up residence in the steeple and gnawed entrances and exits through the shingles to suit their convenience.

And bees built their hives under the wide protecting eaves of the side door of the building. While the steeple was sidelined, a team of roofers got to work applying shingles to the church roof. These shingles were guaranteed by the manufacturer to be raccoon-proof as well as fire proof. One day I drove by and noticed no roofers were working. A week or more passed. Still no work on the roof. Reynolds Carpenter, Junior Warden of the church, explained that the swarms of honeybees which for years had claimed as their own the overhang at the rear door, had objected to the roofing activity and expelled the young men. I went back to see for myself, and sure enough, hardly visible to the casual observer, were huge hives, heavy with honey, hanging above the doors we rarely, if ever, opened.

When the weather cooled off and the bees had calmed down, the roofers returned to finish the job, The crane from Salisbury lifted the steeple back into place. Leaving me still pondering the builders of 1873 and their feat.

We were, however, still without the cross at the top of the steeple. It was finally set in place by a young man in the home repair business whose father was a Mohawk Indian.

Gay Talese wrote a book about the building of the Chesapeake Bay Bridge in which he detailed the role of a tribe of Mohawk Indians of upper New York State in framing its superstructure. This tribe, he explained, is traditionally unafraid of heights and its members are in demand for structural work on skyscrapers.

True to his heritage, their young descendant set up a flimsy ladder one Sunday morning, climbed it cross in hand, and restored it to its place atop the steeple. Just thinking about it made me dizzy. I asked him if there was some trick to keeping steady, balanced. "Well," he said, "you focus on the horizon and never let your eyes waiver." And then, suddenly appalled at his foolhardiness, he admitted: "I must have been crazy. I could have killed myself."

Crane Arrives from Salisbury.

Steeple is now lifted to the ground for repair.

Questions abound:

In 1870, how did the builders solve such problems?

And the cross is still atop the steeple! What happened?

About Weeds, Water Bushes
and Asparagus

On a spring morning I liked to stand framed in one of the long upstairs windows and count my wealth. The dandelions lay thick in the grass like golden coins spilled by some careless Midas. Here and there the honey-heavy dew glinted like diamonds in the sun. I was a miser with never a thought of spending these riches.

When dandelions first bloom they hug the ground on very short stems, avoiding the blades of the mower. As the days pass the stems lengthen and the yellow flowers are transformed into airy silver globes. Children pick them and blow the seed into the air, chanting "one o'clock, (puff) two o'clock, (puff) three o'clock..." And when the last fluffy seed floats away, that's what time it is.

A house guest who once volunteered to "get busy and weed those dandelions out" was astonished at my indignant refusal of her offer.

Weeds. Who's to define them? Suburbanites spend time and money getting rid of dandelions. And a lot of city folk called the bushes that grow thick on the water's edge "water weeds."

This shrub, the Baccharis halimifolia L., grows in profusion in marshes. Our shoreline was thick with the bushes. They like the wet soil at the tide's edge. Cattails spring up among them. They are a favorite nesting place for red-winged blackbirds whose creaky song sounds like an unoiled screen door hinge.

We didn't meddle with our water bushes. They are nature's filtration system. Their shallow roots hold the soil and they protect the shoreline from erosion better than a bulkhead. In August a yellow string-like parasite called dodder writhes throughout the shrub with lethal effect. Known as strangleweed, it wraps its yellow tentacles around stems and branches and chokes them to death.

In spite of their short life span water bushes renew their growth with vigor. I spent many fall afternoons clearing away deadwood and piling the brush into mounds for burning on a windless day. Rabbit hunters would follow their flop-eared beagles, belling after a bunny, on to our property, and complain to me that these piles of brush gave the rabbits a great escape. And, using a turn of phrase peculiar to the area, asked me how I expected them get either rabbit when I was running a reg'lar refuge?

Water bushes bloom profusely in the early autumn putting out white flowers at the tips of each branch. As they fade and die they fill the autumn breezes with fluff, like cottonwood trees or milkweed.

Two women from Connecticut on a sightseeing trip to Old Trinity Church one fall, remarked on their beauty. They were enchanted with this lovely shrubbery blooming so profusely. Where could they get some cuttings to take home? The local women were speechless with astonishment. Only an outsider could find this weedy growth beautiful.

Consider, now, wild asparagus, Mother Nature's gift to the persistent. It came up in early spring, poking its fingers through the leafy loam beneath the honeysuckle hedge where seed had once been dropped by birds. Joe took over the wild asparagus detail and kept a close watch as the shoots began to appear. Their arrival coincided with the spring peepers' song, both harbingers of warm weather, both welcomed by Joe with all his heart. They promised that the cold weather he so dreaded was, for another year at least, a thing of the past.

Asparagus pops up in the same spots year after year. As soon the weather has warmed for a week or two and the rains have softened the earth, the spears begin to push through. If you can catch and harvest them when they are four to six inches high, you have a toothsome dish for the table. And that's the trick. A stalk six inches high and half-inch in diameter is prime eating. But it takes a practiced eye to spot one amid last year's dead grass and the new growth of honeysuckle and poison ivy.

Down on his hands and knees, looking in the secret spots where our asparagus grew, Joe found plenty for our table. But in spite of his best efforts, some always got away. And once asparagus has bolted you have a feathery growth atop a stalk as tough as disappointment.

During its brief season, you can glimpse local folks strolling down the road, their eyes glued to the shoulders where

126

there is low growth. They are looking for wild asparagus, and I wish them luck.

Is it a weed? Well, it is certainly wild. But we owe its presence to the fact that a gentleman named John Hirst III came down to Dorchester County from Elmont, Long Island, in 1890 and cultivated asparagus on 30 to 35 acres on Rose Hill farm which I cannot locate. Other asparagus farms were started, and most of their output was shipped off to Baltimore and New York. Almost a century later, in April 1974, one of John's descendants, Edwin Hirst of Taylor's Island, donated a wooden asparagus buncher to the Farm Museum in Cambridge.

This museum was a pet project of Staplefort Neild, whose barns and sheds at his home, Ridgeton, held quantities of antique farm implements and tools. The original purpose of some of these antiques could present even an expert like Staplefort with a challenge.

I remember his puzzling over one tool -- a strangely curved blade with a sharp end, set into a wooden handle. Baffled, he went to the library to see what he could find. After some painstaking research, he found a picture and description. It was a froe. My dictionary says this tool was designed to "split cask staves and shingles from the block." Cask staves. Who makes casks any more?

It was to house and preserve for posterity artifacts of this sort that Staplefort and his neighbors started the Museum on Taylor's Island. It had been a going concern for a couple of years when Staplefort told me with a laugh: "You know you nearly scared the folks half out of their wits back then, don't you?"

"Scared?" I asked? "Who? When?" And he recalled that I had written an article for the Cambridge paper about the project. Taylor's Island was not used to publicity.

A camera-shy Staplefort Neild stands at the doorway of the school house during a museum open house.

The Taylor's Island Museum

Up and down the county, civic groups were taking over unused school buildings and converting them to community meeting halls. Why leave such a structure to molder when it can be put to good use? And so, the County turned the school house over to a group of residents who organized themselves into the Taylor's Island Community Council.

My nose for news had picked up a scent one day as I drove by the school house, noticed a lot of hustle and bustle and, as is my wont, started asking question. I learned that an energetic group of women was busy washing the many windows and painting the dust-stained walls of the rooms. The men had fixed the roof and made other needed repairs. It was truly a community effort. And I went home and wrote a press release for the *Cambridge Banner* about it.

Not wanting to jump the gun I made several carbon copies -- we are back in the days before I got my first computer -- and delivered one to the home of Reynolds Carpenter whose house stood just across the road from the school building. Reynolds ran a prosperous business raising chickens and selling their eggs. He had been gracious and hospitable to us when we first arrived, inviting us to come to a Whitsunday service at Grace Church and partake of the luncheon afterwards.

Patsy, Reynold's wife, saw me coming up the walkway and called out to her daughter, "Edith! Here comes that awful Mrs. Colic. Run out and see what she wants." She had no notion that I could hear her. All I wanted was to get Reynolds to okay my story. He did, and so did the other leaders of the project.

And the *Cambridge Banner* ran the story and it *was* a little scary because now they were committed and if enthusiasm waned they could scarcely back out of the project.

Then, too, my neighbors were unused to the spotlight publicity can bring. But as time passed they began to enjoy it, then court it, and finally implore me to get them a "free ad" in the paper about a yard sale at the fire house, or a special show at the museum or a ham and oyster supper. And I was usually able to oblige. I even persuaded the *Banner* to run a series of articles I wrote about Patsy Carpenter's role as president of the Dorchester County Homemakers.

And whenever the museum launched a special exhibition the *Banner* obliged with a story that brought people who had never before ventured so far from Cambridge all the way down to Taylor's Island for a look-see.

I wrote about many strange and wonderful contraptions displayed in the museum, but the most curious of all was the tellurian. This was a three-dimensional model of the solar system. Toward the end of the 19th century a tellurian had become a status symbol you displayed in the parlor for your neighbors to marvel at. Like a conch shell.

The one lent to the museum had been built by Jeremiah Spicer, a James Island schoolteacher. Its purpose was to show how the earth and other planets move around the sun. It demonstrated to school children "the causes of day and night and of the seasons." A scientific journal had once called Jeremiah's model "free from defects common to tellurians generally . . ."

David Sears
Chef of many an oyster supper

Oyster Suppers

Oyster flitters. It's the flitters that got 'em. The flitters that filled the fire house for the semiannual oyster suppers, the parking lot jammed and folks lining up outside the door. You may say fritters if you wish. That's all right. I will even give you the recipe. Oysters, of course. You need several gallons, probably ten or more. Shucked.

Then you need lard. Lots of it. I know that today lard is a four-letter word. If you don't believe me, just say it in mixed company and watch folks curl their arms around their middles and cringe.

Next you need cast iron skillets, big, old fashioned black ones.

Now. Take a package of pancake mix -- most any kind will do -- and add whatever it says on the box. Then dump an equal quantity of oysters into the mix, dip out a generous ladle full and pour it into the cast iron skillet where you have melted the lard. I hope you have at least an inch of melted lard in the bottom of the skillet.

Then proceed as if you were making pancakes. You only turn them once. Serve hot, piled high on a platter. One of the volunteers will be waiting to take the flitters to the diners waiting at the tables.

In the meantime these paying guests have been keeping body and soul together with helpings of sliced ham or turkey, homemade potato salad, and string beans out of a can but well seasoned with drippings from the baked hams. Oh yes, there's cole slaw too. Help yourself. Take seconds.

You think eating like that will kill you? Robert Shenton, who worked on the water nearly every day of his life, died at close to a hundred. Jenny Wheatley was ninety or more when she died. They were both wiry; neither one carried an extra ounce of fat. I won't say Julia Child would put one of our recipes on her TV show, but she would certainly say "Pitch in. Eat!" One of Julia's pet peeves is our contemporary fear of food.

Jenny Wheatley used to run the cake table at the suppers. In the early days, when the suppers were first started, the women of the island brought quantities of home-baked cakes and pies -- a boiled milk sponge cake was especially prized. They arrived early in the morning and customers for their wares came early, too, carrying off one of Miss Mabel's coconut cakes or some other specialty.

After dinner, pie was the favorite dessert. School girls pushed carts loaded with slices of apple pie, and lemon meringue, and pumpkin and sweet potato and sold them for a quarter a slice to diners already so full they couldn't force another bite.

That was in the days when there were still a great many women on the island willing to bake. By the time I inherited the job of cake lady from Jenny I noticed a falling off in the number of pies the women brought. So I laid in a supply from the supermarket. If they needed baking I popped them in the oven, several at a time. If they just needed defrosting, that was easy.

Visitors looking over the cake table would ask: "Now whose pie is that?" pointing to one that was clearly mass-produced. And I would smile and answer, "Why that's one of Mrs. Smith's pies." A statement of fact; that was the brand name. Many of Mrs. Smith's pies went home with a happy customer who had paid twice the price of the pie in the store. It was for a good cause. The fire house always needed money.

The twice-yearly oyster suppers on Taylor's Island started at about the time the first volunteer fire company was formed. They were the only fundraiser and they were successful. Staplefort Neild once hinted to me that organizational skills among the residents of the Island were about as low as independence of spirit was high. But order emerged from chaos and David Sears headed up the Taylor's Island Volunteer Fire Company for something like 20 years. While he was in the Army David had been trained as a cook and had a chef's hat to prove it. He knew exactly how to organize these semiannual suppers, how much to buy and how to get the men and women of the Island to pitch in and help out. No mean feat.

Two or three days before the big Saturday the men gathered in a circle in the fire house kitchen and peeled potatoes for the salad. Heads of firm green cabbage waited to be shredded for the slaw. We women cut up the raw potatoes and chopped onions until we wept. And chatted and gossiped and had a good time together. I had learned long since not to introduce any alternate ways of doing things. "That's the way we've always done it," they would tell me, rapping me over the knuckles with a verbal ruler, and that's the way I did it. Mabel Neild took the potatoes home, cooked them and turned them into luscious salad. Before we called it a day we gave the dishes and silver a good washing.

David baked the hams or the turkeys, sitting up all night in the fire house tending the five or six ovens. But he hired cooks to preside over the skillets and fry the flitters during the suppers. They had to be served fresh and hot.

Everybody helped wait on tables. Joe Brown, retired banker and member of a corporate Board of Directors, waited table and bussed. He and I, chatting during slack times, agreed that only in America would you find so many people of such diverse backgrounds volunteering so much of their time for such a project.

Teams of dish washers kept order in the kitchen, running plates and silver through an assembly line that ended with a bath of scalding water. Others dried. We always ran out of dish towels.

The Taylor's Island oyster suppers were famous. People poured in from all over Dorchester County and from as far away as New Jersey. They offered an occasion to spend the day with old friends or family. Folks who had once lived on the Island came down from Baltimore to spend the weekend and help out. The suppers brought old friends and family members together.

The treasurer of the fire company, Thurman Jones, sat at the door and took in the money. At the end of the day when the last diner had waddled out, he'd announce how much had been taken in. A man of few words, he would say: "We made so-and-so much," naming a four-digit figure. Nobody ever asked was that net or gross. Why spoil a great occasion?

Miss Annie's

Miss Annie

David Sears and I were having coffee at the kitchen table. David added two heaping teaspoons of sugar to his cup, poured in some milk, stirred busily and poured out a saucerful. He lifted the saucer to his lips, drank audibly, and set the saucer back down. Not a dropped spilled.

"Miss Annie?" he said. "She musta come down here 25, 30 years ago when she was just a girl. Miz Elliot used to get them girls from the IN-sane Asylum in Cambridge. You know, girls not very smart, left there by their folks? They'd find some place to live and earn their keep doing housework."

David is unraveling a mystery for me. We knew Miss Annie as a very fat woman who lolled on the sagging front porch of a shanty at a busy corner where traffic passed from all directions. Whenever we went by she waddled out to hail us with her urgent cry: "Honey, I just gotta have a cigarette." Her deep voice rasped.

Her sofa had lived through many a winter on the porch and Miss Annie shared it with two or three dogs. Families of cats lived under the porch. The shanty, built of vertical boards, seemed not to belong to anybody.

We always stopped. Miss Annie held out a rough and grimy hand and we give her a fistful of smokes. She wore her stockings just below the knee with a twist intended to help hold them up. Nonetheless, they sagged and her faded cotton dresses emphasized her rolls of fat. And yet, beneath the squalor, a core of dignity shone through. Nobody laughed at Miss Annie.

David continued.

"Back then Annie was a right pretty little thing. Gorman, that's Miz Elliot's boy, wasn't much more than a teenager himself and spoiled to death by his ma. He took a fancy to Annie and they run off and got married.

"Miz Elliot like to bust a gut. Threw 'em both out of the house, and they lived in Gorman's car for a spell. They've been in that shack for a long time. No water, you know. They

135

rigged up a pipe to catch rainwater off the roof." David shrugged. "Don't look like they use much water, anyhow."

David got up and poured himself some hot coffee. He felt at home in our kitchen.

No one seemed to know if Gorman worked or not. He no longer owned a car. He walked the mile or so down to the store and sat around on the bench outside until somebody offered him a ride to town. He was certainly not a very reliable provider; he could disappear for days at a time. What Miss Annie ate and where it came from I never found out. Once when I stopped to hand her some cigarettes, I asked, "Annie, what's your favorite food?"

"Sweet 'tater pie. Yessum. Sweet 'tater pie. That's my favorite."

And, caught up in the spirit of the moment, I sped home and baked one, took it out of the oven and rode back down to the shanty. Nobody was home. I called at the door, "Miss Annie! Miss Annie? I brought you a sweet potato pie." No answer. Nothing stirred, neither dog nor cat nor Annie. I looked around for a place to leave the pie, and found none. No table. If I left it on the porch floor it wouldn't last a minute. I knocked again. I called. Nothing.

I took the pie back home and consoled myself with a large slice.

As time went by Gorman was absent more and more. Miss Annie, her greasy hair growing long, called out to passing cars and waddled over for her cigarettes. That's all she ever asked for.

One day I realized she was gone. An abandoned dog roamed, nose hard to the ground, snuffling for scraps. The sofa was empty. I asked around. It seemed that the public health nurse who stopped by from time to time to check on Miss Annie had recently found her so infested with lice and mange that she wanted to get the poor woman to the Eastern Shore Hospital Center. That's what David had called the IN-sane Asylum.

Nobody would take her there. Nobody wanted this poor derelict woman messing up his nice clean car. Finally, Albert Stanley, our black, one-armed carpenter, rolled her pathetic bulk in a clean sheet, put her in his car, and drove her back to the place she had come from.

Albert Stanley made a comfortable living as a carpenter. He had lost his left arm in the faulty mechanism of a dump truck. The truck had belonged to a taciturn old codger I'll call Jimson. After the accident, Jimson was afraid Albert would go to a lawyer and sue him for all he was worth. So to head off having to pay any damages, he put everything in his wife's name.

Whereupon his wife ran off with another man, taking the money with her. I heard the story told many times and nobody ever expressed the slightest sympathy for the old curmudgeon. He got what he deserved.

Albert, on the other hand, pulled himself together, learned how to use his prosthesis with a shiny metal hook on the end, and found plenty of work. He could set a nail with his good right hand and hammer it in as straight as any two-handed person. He did a lot of carpentering for us. We were pleased with his work and happy to have him come to the house. People liked and respected him. His wife was a handsome woman who drove to her job off the island every day. They owned a neat little house with red carpeting on the living room floor. They earned and held the respect of the entire community.

Elizabeth

My neighbor Elizabeth Ainsworth was a bird. She suffered from osteoporosis, and spent the last days of her ninety-some years in a queenly chair, presiding over her small house on Taylor's Island with a paid companion. The first time I said howdy-do to her, she turned her head away and lifted her nose to the skies. It was not a snub. It was a caricature of a snub. I laughed audibly, wondering what scurrilous tales had inspired her. I got to know her, and learned that to know her was not necessarily to like her. Betty was a woman with a wide contrary streak. If you said you had sweet potatoes for dinner she would say with a little simper: "You mean yams, don't you?" If you said there was a power failure she would suggest that you had really meant to say "power outage," the correct term. Well, to me it was a failure and never mind the electric company's jargon.

We had a power failure one November when a strange, late-arriving hurricane hit. The winds had bypassed our area, but the storm had pushed about ten inches of water over the Island. Our house, perched on its invisible hill, was dry. But I worried about Betty. I knew her electric stove wasn't working. And her telephone was out, too.

Betty was born in Philadelphia, the daughter of a policeman killed in the line of duty whose heroism is memorialized, along with others, on a plaque in Washington, D. C. Redheaded and petite, she caught the eye of Royce Ainsworth, an Air Force flyer, and they were married. When Royce retired they bought a small house on a large piece of low-lying waterfront property on Taylor's Island. I knew her lane would likely be flooded.

But it t was not just altruism that set me out on my expedition. I was curious to see the extent of the flooding, and exploring by car was out of the question. I filled a thermos with hot coffee, freshly brewed on our stove fueled by propane gas, and set out on foot to see what there was to see.

It was a two-mile walk to Betty's, maybe a little more. I had done it often in dry weather, but this time was different. I put on boots and a sweater -- for November the air was unusually balmy -- and set out. By the time I got to the end of our lane and turned on to Pine Top Road water was running into my boots and it was cold.

I slogged on, more and more water sloshing over my boot tops. I promised myself that when I got to the first house along the way I'd sit on the steps and empty them. The steps, when I got there, were under water.

Nothing to do but keep sloshing along. I made it to Betty's house where a bench on her porch was reasonably dry and I got the boots off, knocked and entered, barefoot, with my thermos. She was very glad to see somebody, took the thermos of coffee, and said: "I hope it's cocoa."

While I was sitting for a spell to catch my breath, a repair truck from the electric company arrived, reconnected Betty's electricity and knocked on the door to inquire where the Kroliks or Cowlicks or something like that lived. I said I'd be delighted to show them the way, piled into their truck sitting high on mag wheels and got a ride home. The crew was impressed that I had walked all that distance. In retrospect, I was, too.

At home, Joe had a pot of hot coffee going. The linemen soon had us fixed up with electricity. They came in and we all sat around the kitchen table and celebrated with a slice of toasted pound cake and strong, hot coffee. Nobody wanted cocoa.

Unten

Unten. It's German. And it doesn't simply mean "under." It's "below," as in below the salt. You get the implication -- it is demeaning. And "unten" was the unofficial designation of Yugoslav lands in German speaking countries. In Austria it was especially honored. Unten -- beneath contempt. You don't want to go there.

Shopping in Vienna in 1956 for a red velvet evening dress to wear to a special New Year's Eve party in Belgrade, I explained to the seamstress that I needed a rush job on the alterations because in a couple of days I was returning home to Belgrade.

"Ach!" She was sympathetic. She commiserated. "Poor thing. Unten. . . . " I know she pictured a dreadful life surrounded by poverty and disagreeable people. That was the stereotype. She had, of course, never been there.

A couple we knew some years later in Bonn, Germany, were being assigned to Belgrade -- he, for the newspaper he worked for. His German-born wife was distraught at the prospect of life "unten." Their farewell party was more a wake than a celebration. Not a year later, gossip had it that she had abandoned her American husband and run off with a Serb, and my dear, a one-armed man at that.

It took my husband Joe and me some time to realize that Taylor's Island was "Unten" to the rest of Dorchester County. Buying a ride-on mower at the Cambridge hardware store, we wrote our check for $800 and asked to have the machine delivered to Taylor's Island. The young salesman was flabbergasted. "Taylor's Island? You want it delivered to Taylor's Island? Well, I don't know. That might could cost extra." "It's not in West Virginia," I snapped and learned that such a comeback was even more off-putting than the fact that we lived on Taylor's Island. Women on the Eastern Shore of Maryland are not given to that kind of repartee.

Then there was Caroline Todd, a woman of means and social standing, if not popularity, who lived in Cambridge. She telephoned me one day, although Caroline scarcely needed a phone. "Why do you live down there on Taylor's Island?" she bawled. "There's nothing but idiots live down there." Unten! Caroline could rattle Mt. Rushmore. She rattled me. If I had had my wits about me, I'd have said: "Well, Caroline, there you have it." But *le mot juste* escaped me. I doubt Caroline Todd had ever set foot on the Island. But she knew, nonetheless.

I have one more, and that's all:

One Saturday afternoon our little family -- my husband, our daughter and I -- washed, combed and nicely dressed, boarded a bus for a Baltimore dinner theater. The women of the Episcopal Church in Cambridge arranged these trips as a fund-raising enterprise and we enjoyed going. At the theater we took our places at a table with two pouter-pigeon matrons from Cambridge. We exchanged pleasantries, and the women asked where we lived. We said Taylor's Island. The two exchanged glances and smiled in unison. They knew a joke when they heard one. "No. No," they protested. "Where do you *really* come from?"

But coins have heads, as well as tails. Shopping in New York or in Washington, at Saks Fifth Avenue or the late Garfinckel's, Mary and I often asked to have our purchases mailed to us.. We blithely gave our address as Taylor's Island, Md. And with pencil poised, the saleswomen waited for the rest. We gave the zip. "That's all? Oh, my goodness! You actually LIVE on an island. That's so *Interesting!* Really!" The most sophisticated, soignee saleswomen grew wide-eyed at the very thought. Yes, we actually *lived* on an island.

There were, unfortunately, economic as well as social implications to this "unten" business. Parts of the Island started experiencing electrical failures on summer weekends, caused, we suspected, by the fact that campers renting trailers at a camp ground on the Bay shore came in from swimming and boating between 5 and 6, turned on the air conditioners, and ZAP! The circuit was overloaded. Some people got mad with the camp ground. I got mad with Choptank Electric, which I had long suspected underestimated the demand for electricity on the Island.

I wrote a letter to our state senator, Fred Malkus, who replied, in effect, that we ought to be grateful to have *any* electricity on Taylor's Island at all. And if it hadn't been for FDR's Rural Electrictrification Administration we *wouldn't have* had any. "Unten," again.

After I posted his letter in the window of the Island store, he did a quick about face. But that's another story.

Osprey poised to dive for a fish

Birds

Osprey

Travers Spicer and his wife, Bobby -- she of the Christmas tree lights   -- lived in one of the island's older houses called Oyster Creek Farm, not far from Mulberry Grove.   The renovation bug bit Trav, as he was known, and he installed picture windows in the old place which gave a nice view over Oyster Creek.   He upgraded the plumbing, too, but he never quite got around to updating the heating system.

Just as he never got around to keeping the unique five-hole privy from falling down although some architecture buffs had offered to take it off his hands as a museum piece.   The facility boasted three small holes for the children and two large one for parents.   It was a frame structure dating from the early nineteenth century, originally located at Mulberry Grove.   "The privy is of such quality as to make it rare in the state of Maryland," according to the editors of *Between the Nanticoke and the Choptank, An Architectural History of Dorchester County, Maryland.*

When Trav died, Bobby soldiered on alone in the house, learning to coax the old stoves into keeping her warm during the winter.   Their mechanism was complicated and each of them was connected by a stovepipe to its own chimney.   A proper draft was essential.

On the opposite side of the Island, Joe and Elizabeth Browne had built a handsome brick house overlooking the Little Choptank River.   Joe was a retired Baltimore banker "who wanted to try his hand at farming," he once told me. Elizabeth was a Baltimore belle of the old school who could have made Emily Post look gauche.   Elizabeth knew to the minutes when it was proper to put on dangling earrings (certainly not before 6 p.m.), and the precise moment as summer ended to stop wearing white shoes.   Elizabeth, personally, did an enormous amount of successful gardening. The farming, for the most part, fell to David Sears.

145

Joe Browne was an outdoors man, a hunter, a sports fan. He would gather up a few local friends and drive to Baltimore to a ball game.   Elizabeth preferred to be within   driving distance of one of Elizabeth Arden's Red Doors.

But she found much to hold her interest on Taylor's Island. Ospreys, for instance. She had a platform built off shore at a spot she could easily see from her den on the second floor of their house. (The first floor was set aside for visiting family and there was an elevator.)

To this platform, every year without fail, the osprey returned on March 17 to the nest they had built there.   The birds never disappointed.   Once arrived, they lost no time making repairs and renovations to the old nest, lining it with dried seaweed they found in fluffy windrows on the beach. Elizabeth cheered her pair on, delighted with the progress they were making with their renovations.   Field glasses ever at the ready, she soon spotted an egg.   Three eggs completed the clutch. All three hatched.

Ospreys are fish eaters. They fly over the water from a great height until they spot a fish, trail it, then dive at high speeds emerging with the fish between both claws. They shake themselves off and return to the nest. Elizabeth told me how the mother bird teaches this technique to each of her young, coaching them until they have got it down pat.

One year, though, Elizabeth said, the third hatchling couldn't seem to master the technique: fly high, look down, spot fish, swoop, snatch it. Oops! Missed! Try again. And again. Elizabeth watched for days as the mother bird persisted, until, at last, the youngster caught on.

Soon thereafter her osprey family were gone, flying down to South America to winter warmly, south of the equator.

Bobby Spicer's experience with the fish hawks, as the birds were know locally was quite different from Elizabeth Browne's.

Ospreys are big birds, about two feet long with wide wingspans. They always build their bulky nests of twigs near the water. You will find them, for instance, nesting on channel markers. A chimney on an old house by the water serves very well, too. One March a persistent pair of nesting birds spotted a likely looking chimney on Bobby's house on Oyster Cove.

And when Bobby noticed that a fish hawk was piling nesting material on top of her living room chimney she took alarm. Understandably. Good heavens, a nest on the chimney would ruin the draft and could even cause a fire.

She called for help to the Blackwater Wildlife Refuge whose naturalists were generous with their expertise. Bobby's query, however, seemed to stump them. The best they could do was suggest she honk the horn of her car to frighten the birds away. Early the next morning Bobby maneuvered her Buick to a good watching spot and began her vigil. And here they came, confounded fish hawks, claws laden with bundles of twigs. Bobby beeped the horn. No result. She beeped twice. Again, no result. Dog-gone it! She leaned on the horn, blasting the neighborhood, and the birds flew away. But not for long. Soon they were back with another load of twigs. Again Bobby, who was developing a painful crick in her neck, tooted the horn. She leaned on the horn, not once, not twice, but again and again. She kept her vigil until she was sure the birds had quit for the day.

It took several days of violent horn attacks to finally convince this pair of stubborn ospreys that Bobby's chimney was not a fit place to build a home and raise a family.

Humble Pie

The great blue heron is a patient fisherman, waiting in the shallows to snatch a fat minnow or a small bluegill in his long pointed bill. This bird can stand as high as four feet tall, counting his long legs and neck. His feathers are a bluish gray, and standing on one leg at the edge of the marsh, he is the picture of dignity. A great blue frequented the fringes of our reedy shore and we were flattered to have his company.

Our heron especially liked to fish the waters of the tidal ditch that separated the Pine Top Road from our soy bean field, his beady eye scanning the water, his long neck poised to lunge. Our car always spooked him, and we liked to watch him rise, his great wings pumping in the effort to lift his bulk up, up, and take to the air. After a few furious flaps, he would rise and sail ahead of us down the road, his wings now gently fanning the air, his long legs trailing behind. The loblolly pines that lined the road offered no opening for his wide wingspan and we moseyed along behind him until he found a gap and veered into the woods.

One day, mosey was not in my vocabulary. I was full of important errands and appointments in Cambridge, and the heron's leisurely pace chafed. For once I sped up and drove directly under him. It frightened him. It literally scared the stuffing out of him. A torrent of bird lime rained down on the roof of the car, slithered over the windshield, dirtied the windows. All my sense of importance and bustle evaporated. I took the first opportunity to turn around and head back home.

Half an hour later, the car hosed down and in condition to appear in polite society, I started out all over again, chewing on my slice of humble pie.

Quail

If you have never walked up a narrow lane far out in the country with no noisy traffic, no bustle of crowds, no sound at all, kicking an oyster shell, thinking about hot soup for lunch, and POW! there is a sudden explosion at your feet and a covey of quail rises from a bush and flies away -- if you have never had this experience you cannot know the heart-stopping excitement the moment brings.

Quail are oval in shape, ground birds, walkers, members of the chicken family. Their feathers are the color of pecans. When they decide to take wing, a rising covey makes a distinctive whirring sound as the birds scamper through the air to find new cover. Quail are also known as partridges or bobwhites after the sound of their sweet whistle.

Joe and I were still new to the house when, one morning shortly after dawn with a hint of autumn in the air, we saw out the kitchen window a mother quail strutting along, hugging the bushes that lined the water's edge. She had six chicks in tow. Five were symmetrically arranged in a row like tin soldiers, tagging along as if it were a game of Follow the Leader. Which is exactly what it was.

Mother set the pace and the example. She walked sedately, pausing now and then to relish a seed from the grasses. The Five marched right behind, stopping when Mother stopped, walking when Mother walked. Number six, though, dawdled, kept to no straight line and stopped to look over his shoulder. Enter Father, swooping low over the straggler who hurried to join the ranks.

But soon he lagged behind again. This time when Father swooped down with a whirr Number Six lost his balance and did a somersault. Then, his legs pumping -- quail walk just like chickens -- he got back into line.

Joe and I held our breath hardly daring to move lest a shadow spook the birds. Mother Quail worked the length of the grassy stretch, always close to the edge of the water bushes. She turned a corner, heading away from the creek, still hugging the low growth.

Suddenly her mate whistled "Bob White" once from the honeysuckle vines and Mother and Six vanished into the leafy cover as if a magician had waved his wand. And although we hoped to, we never saw such a show again.

Osprey holding caught fish in its talons

Me and Snakes

The Big Broad in the comic strip B.C. takes a stick to the snake. And while she and I have much in common, I take a different approach. Call it live and let live. Our house was home to numerous black snakes, also called Racers. They wintered in the insulation beneath the attic floor, snuggled down against the cold. These harmless creatures grow to six or seven feet in length and shed their skins in spring. You could find three or four such sheds in our attic every year.

We also enjoyed visits from smaller snakes. Late one night my husband, the insomniac, was reading in the kitchen when a skinny little fellow about 12 inches long crept out from beneath the baseboard heating element. Joe took a broom to it and managed to give it a hefty thwack before it slithered away. A few nights later it came out again to explore our kitchen, this time with a bend in its middle, and we caught it and put it in a jar with holes poked in the lid.

What kind of snake was it? We needed to know, and I took the jar down to the country store   where the nature boys hung out afternoons, plunked it down on the bar and said, "Anybody know what kind of snake this is?"

Nobody did. One older man lifted the lid from the jar and sniffed and said, "Smells like vinegar. Sure sign of a copperhead. Lady you got a copperhead snake in there. Yes indeedy."

"Oh, good grief! It's a pickle jar," I said.

Another patron, rising from his bar stool, inched closer to me.

"Lady, it's none of my business," he whispered. "But I would get out of that house and never go back. You don't catch me living with no snakes."

A third gentler type sipped his beer, contemplated the poor snake and said, "He's shore little, ain't he?"

On the way home I stopped by the post office where I ran into a neighbor who worked at the Blackwater Wildlife Refuge. He didn't know what kind of snake it was either, but suggested we take it to the Refuge and ask one of the naturalists on the staff.

The following day, Joe did just that. He returned with an empty jar and said our snake was nothing but a harmless little old milk snake. The naturalist at Blackwater explained that milk snakes like to nest in old houses.

Nest? Yes. We saw more of these peaceful little creatures once in a while and they caused us no further concern. However, one sunny afternoon I had just finished tidying the guest room in preparation for a visit from Jennifer, a city friend of mine. And there, lolling peacefully on the molding above the door, its head dangling toward the left, its tail hanging limply down toward the right, was a milk snake. I could imagine Jennifer's shrieks as she started to walk through the door and spotted this baby. I could picture her grabbing her overnight bag and high-tailing it down the lane in her Honda, spraying gravel every which way. I got a pencil and a jar, carefully eased the little snake into it, and carried him outside. You see, I could never bring myself to touch a snake. Not even a little old milk snake.

Boats

"There is nothing -- absolutely nothing -- half so much worth doing as simply messing about in boats."
-- Water Rat in *Wind in the Willows.*

The entire Kolarek family embraced this philosophy. In 1970, once Joe had retired and we were back home for good, our first priority was to buy Mary a present for her thirteenth birthday -- a skiff of her own, a flat-bottom row boat about 12-feet long which her father christened "The Queen Mary" with a bottle of creek water.

I loved nice stable flat-bottomed wooden row boats, loved fitting a well-balanced pair of oars with their oarlocks into the tholes and sweeping out into the wind and current. I soon learned that the hubris of rowing along with the tide and wind came to an embarrassing end when I turned around to head home. In the exhilaration, the confidence, as the shore goes flying by and the oars cut the water to great effect, you forget that most of the work is being done by an outgoing tide and the wind at your back.

Alas alack, the journey home can be long and arduous, can leave you winded, humbled, with palms blistered. On one such occasion, exhausted and out of patience with my lack of discernable progress, I headed into the reeds, left the boat half in and half out of the water, threw out an anchor and walked home through the marsh, stepping on an indignant black snake napping in the sun en route.

Mary took responsibility for maintaining her boat, scraping the barnacles off the bottom each spring -- copper paint helped protect against this pest, but was not a 100 percent guarantee -- caulking it and giving it a fresh coat of paint. One year she painted the boat blue, just for variety's sake, and learned from the local watermen that you must never, never paint a boat blue. You are courting disaster. We were never concerned about Mary when she went out on the water. She was a good swimmer and Slaughter Creek, except for the channel, was not too deep. We considered her a strong, competent oarswoman with good judgment. The blue-boat jinx never touched her.

And then there was the sailboat. Once he had retired, Joe resolved to teach himself how to sail. He bought and devoured books on the subject, got the vocabulary down pat, and eventually located a sailboat he felt he could afford. It had been built by a young man born on Taylor's Island to a prominent farm family. Boats were not in his blood, and the end product proved the point. This large wooden structure did, in fact, float on the surface of the water, but she was as hard to sail as a cast iron skillet.

In spite of all the skills he had absorbed from his books, Joe ran aground, got tangled up in overhanging trees, bumped into the pier at the marina across the creek, and generally had a bad time. I kept an eye across the water and when he was overdue I would hop in a skiff and row out to find him. I never got the knack of making the outboard motor turn over, and stopped trying. I enjoyed rowing. Finding Joe wasn't difficult. He never got far from home. We started calling the sailboat The Tub.

Joe finally realized he would never get anywhere trying to sail this unwieldy craft, especially not in a narrow body of water with fluky winds like Slaughter Creek. He bought a 14-foot Penguin and sailed it very well.

The Tub, tied up off our shoreline, was the embodiment of inertia. At rest, she was determined to remain at rest. In motion, look out. Hauling her out of the water come cold weather, and launching her again in spring, became a serious problem. Joe decided to get rid of her. He hoped word of mouth would produce a taker. Nothing. He bought classified ads in the Cambridge paper. No takers. For a couple of years she sat in front of our house, in and out of the water, unused, an eyesore in need of paint. We were stuck with her. Late one October when we had tried unsuccessfully for weeks to find somebody to help us haul her ashore, she was still in the water and we were in despair.

October is a month when the moon and the sun and the earth line up in a tidy row -- there are words like syzygy, apogee and perigee that properly describe the situation. When this happens tides are apt to run ultra high. Predictions of high water did not always result in high water, however, and we tended to be cavalier about syzygies. But late one October afternoon when I was driving down alone from Columbia to spend a weekend at the house, the water was indeed very high. All along my route the ditches were full to overflowing and I splashed through water on low spots along the road.

I worried a little about a stretch near Cator Cove some two miles from home. It always flooded under such circumstances. Sure enough, it was under water, a lot of water; I must have arrived at about flood tide. The growths of tall marsh grass on the verges were my only clue as to where the road lay.

All my "can do" impulses kicked in and I edged my way slowly along. Slowly, slowly. Don't slosh, don't get the engine wet. I knew that once launched on this course of action I could not turn around. The road was just about wide enough for two cars to pass.

Two inches of water. Four inches of water. Six inches of water. And more water. Whooo. This is tricky. What am I doing driving around in the middle of Chesapeake Bay? Back up? Impossible now. Just go slow, keep your eyes on that grass, girl. Don't lose the road. A short dicey stretch, my palms sweating, put me in the clear and homeward bound. En route I made a plan. I knew our front yard would be covered in four to six inches of water. The Tub would follow me like a hungry puppy if I pulled her ashore. It was worth a try.

I rushed into the house, tore off my sweater and skirt and headed toward the water in my underwear. Night was falling fast. No time to struggle into a bathing suit. The water was very cold. I knew it would be, threw myself in and got past that shock. The Tub followed me -- just like a puppy. I brought her easily ashore and tied her up to a stake.

I prayed no Good Samaritan from the Coast Guard Station across the creek would spot me in my sopping undies and rush over to help. The *Queen Mary* and the second rowboat were no problem. I tied them up, and awash in pride, went in the house, had a hot shower and enjoyed a stiff drink.

The Tub sat in the yard where I had secured her for a year or more, on the verge of becoming a derelict. Finally we persuaded a neighbor to come and haul her away. We gladly paid his hefty fee and said good riddance.

Oyster boats on Slaughter Creek.
Below, a waterman tonging for oysters.

Delicacies

A Muzzle of Oysters

The older men liked to reminisce about how they'd gather around the polling place on Election Day and enjoy a muzzle of oysters and talk politics. They would tell me this slyly, waiting for me to ask: "A muzzle? -- of oysters?" and then explain. The muzzle was made out of chicken wire shaped to fit over a horse's nose to keep it from nibbling the corn or other crops during harvest time. In the winter it was filled with oysters and dipped into a pot of boiling water. After a minute or two the oysters would begin to open, and could be enjoyed on the spot. A quarter would get you all you could eat.

We were still new to the ways of the water when we woke early one October morning to see Slaughter Creek covered with the workboats of watermen tonging for oysters on the first day of the season.

I explain what oyster tongs look like in the chapter about James Island. But you really have to be there. That morning Joe grabbed a camera, we got into a skiff and ventured out, snapping pictures of men standing on the gunwales of their work boats, dipping their long-handled tongs into the depths, working them together like tin snips chewing at a stubborn piece of metal, and bringing them up, hand-over-hand, their rake-like ends enclosing a mass of oysters.

Here's a strange bit of lore a waterman once told me. If you go out and buy a bushel of oysters and bring them home with you, and wonder where you can best keep them fresh, and decide to put them back down in the cool February water beneath your pier and go back into the house, don't be surprised if you return to find them gone. That's right. Once you have put them back into the water, even in the shadow of your own pier, they are public property and anyone may walk away with them. Be warned.

Muskrats

Then there are muskrats. These aquatic mammals live in marshes, are excellent swimmers and can stay under water for as long as 15 minutes. Their pelt is a saleable fur made into ladies' coats, sometimes dyed to look like something else more expensive. When we lived on Taylor's Island muskrat meat was abundant during January when trappers could take them for their fur. The muskrat itself was a leftover which sold in markets for something like a dollar apiece. The meat is laced with tiny white musk glands that have to be dug out and discarded; otherwise the cooked meat is not palatable. They were a delicacy I came to enjoy, if somebody else cleaned and cooked them. Properly prepared the meat tastes like gamey dark-meat chicken. I find it delicious.

I recently made friends with a young city-bred couple who enjoy entertaining and like to serve exotic dishes. The hostess dares her guests to try one of her specialties: "If you thought you'd never put such-and-such in your mouth, well just try this," she challenges, proffering a dish. After polishing off one of her concoctions I put down my empty plate and asked:

"Do you like muskrat?" If you want to bring thundering silence into a room, these four words will do it.

P.S. People of true refinement on the Eastern Shore who eat muskrat, call it marsh rabbit.

Black Bass from the Gunpowder River

For recreation, Joe depended heavily on fishing for large mouth black bass. He had his choice of three rivers, the Chicamacomico, the Transquaking or the Blackwater. All three were brackish -- neither fresh nor salt -- somewhere in between.

The Blackwater was closest, about 15 miles from our house, and for several summers Joe kept a wooden skiff anchored at the river. He paid a dollar a week for the privilege, and the property owner was happy to see him coming. Once in a while I spent a day on the Blackwater with Joe. In this green, remote watery world I felt a million miles away from cities, towns, people, cars -- you could believe nothing had changed since the beginning of time.

Five large mouth black bass per day was the limit a fisherman was allowed to take, and once in a while Joe was able to catch that many. A friend had taught me how to fillet fish and with practice I became accomplished and proud of my skill. My two very sharp wooden-handled Finnish knives especially designed for the purpose made the job easy.

We usually had a good backlog in our freezer, but fresh out of the water, when the flavor is at its peak, is the best way to eat this, or any, fish. Black bass is a game fish not found on the market. It is nothing at all like the salt-water sea bass and shouldn't be confused with it.

Deer Season

Venison is something you will not find on the market, either, and it came my way infrequently. If young neighbors complained about growing tired of the deer meat in their freezer, I'd offer to swap them a couple of T-bone steaks for some venison.

Dorchester County, during deer season -- the week toward the end of November when you can use a rifle as opposed to bow and arrow -- is overrun with young men who come down from the suburbs of Baltimore, rough it, let their beards grow and their clothes get dirty, and perch for hours in a deer stand, just sitting, and waiting for a deer to come by. A deer stand is nothing more than a wooden platform nailed together high up in a tree. A young woman whose husband was a passionate hunter complained to me that he put his clothes into a gunnysack full of overripe apples for several days before deer season. This was supposed to mask his human smell.

We had our share of hunters on Taylor's Island, but they respected our privacy. Walking our two dogs, however, I wore a red flannel shirt and, from time to time shouted, "Don't shoot my dogs, please."

Here I have a word for my city friends who may be cringing at the thought of this "slaughter." Our advertising artists -- along with Mr. Disney's animators -- have sold us a mischievously false picture of Mother Nature as a handsome Junoesque woman wearing a wreath of flowers on her brow, surrounded by adorable creatures all loving each other, all just begging to be picked up and cuddled.

Erase this picture from your mind. Mother nature is a powerful force who always gets her way. In her food chain the spiders are eating the mosquitoes (which can bite a man to death); the robins are eating the worms; the cats are after the robins and the owls are after the kittens and robins. The hawks are after the mice and voles, the rabbits, vegetarians, themselves, are fair game to foxes and hawks; the dogs are chasing raccoons, the osprey are diving for fish, the big fish eat the little fish and so it goes up and down the food chain to the man out after his deer to feed his family.

Tomatoes

If you are one of those poor, deprived souls who thinks of tomatoes as pale reddish vegetables with the flavor of wet blotting paper, you clearly have never set foot on the Eastern Shore of Maryland in the summertime. There is something in the soil there that gives tomatoes a special tangy flavor. Which may have been why tomatoes canned there were popular wherever they were shipped.

But the times, they were a-changing and canneries were going out of business. At the end of World War II with the sweet smell of prosperity in the air, it was virtually impossible to find youngsters who would spend a day bending over in the fields to set out young plants in straight rows, let alone for the dollar a day Bill Keene once earned for that work.

Settling on the Island after the war on Oyster Creek Farm, next door to Mulberry Grove, Travers and Bobby Spicer expected to work the family farm and were ill prepared for a generation of teenagers who spurned an offer of 50 cents an hour for this monotonous, tiring work. Bobby often told me about her frustration, trying to recruit boys to come down to the farm and set out tomato seedlings. "Even," as she once said petulantly, "even when I'd go get 'em in my car and drive 'em back home again."

Picking was done by hand, too. Men in their seventies look back with a shudder at picking tomatoes when they were teenagers. "Early in the morning the vines were wet with dew and your clothes were soon soaked. Then the mosquitoes descended. If you fought off the mosquitoes you couldn't pick. The sun rose high in the sky and you began to swelter and itch unbearably. Then your back began to ache. And sometimes, you just walked off the job."

Small wonder that commercial tomato production began to lose favor. When we first started our treks to Taylor's Island in 1960 there were still a few canneries operating and we became familiar with the unmistakable sour odor of rotting tomato peels in late summer as we drove through the night. One cannery was on the outskirts of Cambridge, one was near Church Creek and the last, at Woolford. Soon, all of them vanished.

Today, growing tomatoes commercially has just about disappeared in Dorchester County. But gardeners there still grow the best tomatoes in the world. Even I produced crops of wonderful, tasty, juicy, bright red tomatoes.

Debate rages over the most flavorful variety. I favored Rutgers, but others said it was too susceptible to disease. Then the Big Boy varieties that produced enormous fruit were introduced. Whatever you planted, it was hard to go wrong. I miss those tomatoes. No roadside stand, no grocery store, offers fruit anywhere near as full of flavor as the tomatoes that grow on the Eastern Shore. Let me narrow that down to the tomatoes that grow on Taylor's Island.

Just walk out the kitchen door when the sun has warmed the face of the earth. Take a salt shaker if you think of it, but that's not essential. Pick one of those bright red globes and bite into it. The juice will squirt out and run down your clothes but that doesn't matter. The flavor is as exciting as a first kiss.

The Message in the Bottle

Say our house dated from 1815, a likely year for all three pieces to have been brought together to form a single dwelling, and for the owner to have built a pier out over the water. The pier was as necessary as the "necessary." A long pier provided a place to tie up a boat at low tide. Ours extended out 25 or 30 feet. When we first bought the house in 1960 there was a heavy growth of seaweed around the shore line and when we got into our skiff in those days, we had to row beyond this grass before we could put the outboard motor into the water.

The pier served yet another purpose. You took anything that could not be burned, mulched or fed to the pigs out to the end and dumped it overboard. And it sank out of sight into the grass or the muddy bottom. As a consequence, today we enjoy a heritage of bottles, jars and pottery shards that tell a lot about the way people used to live. The fragments of the china sugar bowl secretly jettisoned, the shards of the butter crock that fell and smashed, the ears from teacups. And the empty bottles -- the vanilla bottles, the Bromo-Seltzer bottles, the baking powder bottles, bottles of every sort you can imagine, all survived.

Within a few years of our arrival, the seaweed disappeared. Why it did is another story; I think the question remains unanswered. It was then that I started clearing a spot along the shoreline where we could walk out into the water without cutting our feet on 150 years' accumulation of crockery shards and pieces of broken glass. Soon I began finding unbroken bottles. One of the first was a vanilla bottle. I recognized it instantly, although the water and the years had turned it the bluish color of skim milk.

My mother had bought vanilla in exactly that kind of corked bottle when I was a little girl. A Southern belle of no mechanical skill, it took all her patience and ingenuity to dig that little cork out of the narrow neck of the bottle. She attacked it with an ice pick. And when the cork was at last, destroyed, the problem remained of how to reclose the bottle.

I found myself not just keeping the bottles I found in Slaughter Creek. I sensed that I was beginning to collect them.

163

I tended to cull them out -- those that originally held cork stoppers I classified as "old," a highly subjective term, and those with screw tops were new and uninteresting. And I got intrigued. Like old documents, these bottles were a window into the lives of the people who had gone before us.

If necessity is the mother of invention, scarcity is the mother of thrift. All the bottles I retrieved have one thing in common -- they are small. This may be because smaller bottles survived whereas larger ones broke more readily. Or perhaps the bigger bottles were kept and used over and over again. To buy a small amount of whiskey, you took your own bottle. But I think the answer is that the day of "large," "giant" and "monster" sizes lay in the distant future. Thrift governed the size of the bottles that made their way to market.

After the squatty little Bromo-Seltzer bottles, McCormick's vanilla bottles were the most common. I found a great many of them, flat little things holding at most eight teaspoonsful.   A relationship between the two has been suggested, but remains undocumented. The story goes that a bottle of vanilla provided a potent potable in the absence of liquor. And the Bromo-Seltzer was an effective hangover remedy. And a superstition that Bromo- Seltzer was effective as a male birth control medium was also whispered about. The ubiquitous Bromo-Seltzer bottles deserve their own chapter.

Next come the Rumford Baking Powder bottles, six inches high, round shouldered, with chunky necks that once held a cork. In our home, where my mother baked biscuits from scratch all the time, baking powder came in cans. But the women of the Island, like Laura Navy's mother who produced huge quantities of biscuit, were obviously committed to Rumford's.

Chas. H. Fletcher's Castoria was a popular remedy for colicky children. And Groves Tasteless Chill Tonic prepared by Paris Medicine Co., St. Louis, -- all data embossed on the bottle I found -- was another well-known cure. The meticulous observation of good usage on Hence Bro's & White Philadelphia, endears another bottle.   The apostrophe is included in the name embossed on its side. But I have no idea what it contained, like the one labeled "O.F. Woodward, Leroy, N. Y. " The Woodward family of Leroy, N. Y. developed Jell-O and prospered. But what did they put in bottles so long ago?

Souvenirs of early cosmetics turned up, too. I have kept one that held Hind's Honey and Almond Cream, a popular lotion for chapped hands, like Glycerin and Rosewater. Jergens lotion and Woodbury's and Pond's face creams found favor with ladies of the Island. And then there is the small flat white glass jar that contained Mum, one of the earliest underarm deodorants to appear on the market. A copy of Delineator magazine for March, 1907 -- a woman's magazine of an era when many such publications prospered -- contains an advertisement for Mum. It promised to keep one "dainty." The product used the advertising slogan "Mum's the Word," a precursor of the use of the word Secret on a more recent product.

Dear to my heart is an old inkwell, sand-scoured, and missing a little chunk out of the back, but I keep it turned around so the hole doesn't show. It bears no marking but its shape takes me back to paintings of the founding fathers dipping a quill into an inkwell. And I have a Watermen's Ink bottle, the kind we plunged our fountain pens into to fill the little rubber reservoir.

Separating the cork-stoppered from the "new" screw capped bottles led me to speculate when the screw cap gained favor. I know vanilla bottles continued to be corked until the 1920s. On my windowsill are three old Mason Ball jars, none of which, incidentally, was found in the creek. One is embossed with the date 1858, the date the screw cap for canning jars was patented. Did the smaller bottling companies have to wait for a patent to expire before they could use screw caps on their bottles? I wonder.

A trio of Nehi soda pop bottles worked their way into my collection. They were found in a field where a couple of milk bottles also turned up -- quart milk bottles, once closed with a little cardboard tab. When the milk bottles stood on the doorstep outside our house in the city on a very cold morning, the cream at the top froze and expanded, and the little caps rose as if saluting winter.

Pawnee Indian Relief

Low tides are like strippers, laying bare the creek bed, inviting the eye to have a look.   I stood at the end of our pier one cold February morning looking out over mud flats I had never explored.   Now they lay exposed and in the distance I saw something glinting.   It looked like a bottle.   I would have to go and take a closer look.   Walking across this muddy flat demanded special skills.   As you stepped into the sticky goo, you could hear it suck at your footwear.   If you had on boots or galoshes they sank into the mud and stayed there.   When you pulled they came squooshing out suddenly, upsetting your already precarious balance, and down you went.

In the garage I found a pair of old tennis shoes, stained veterans of many such trips, tied them tightly around my feet and stepped out. The water was icy. After a few steps my feet grew numb.   The bottle was a long way off. The creek bottom made gulping sounds with each step.   Squelch, squelch, squelch, I made my way out to where my trophy lay half buried in the mud.

It was a cylindrical bottle four inches long and an inch in diameter.   It was in fine shape, not a crack, not a chip. Embossed on its side were the words "Pawnee Indian Relief." It had once held 12 teaspoonsful of the mixture, and was a stoppered bottle. Pawnee Indian Relief! Quackery epitomized. Heading back to shore, slowly, one frozen foot after the other, I pictured a snake oil merchant standing on the flatbed of a wagon above the expectant faces of country folk in town on a Saturday.   Maybe he had a tame Indian wearing an elaborate feathered headdress as a prop.   And he promised a cure for everything from corns to baldness -- rheumatism, colic, constipation, diarrhea.

"Only one dollar. Step right up, folks." He probably did very well. The name of his product was compelling. And the first dose of what was probably largely alcohol, undoubtedly produced an agreeable buzz. By the time I got it back to my warm kitchen, I, too, would have welcomed a swig of Pawnee Indian Relief from a freshly uncorked bottle.

Joe Browne and Blue Glass Bottles

When Isaac Emerson, a   Baltimore pharmacist, developed Bromo-Seltzer he knew his product was volatile and needed a container that would protect it from light rays. He ordered blue glass bottles from a New Jersey company but his product became so popular so fast that the manufacturer couldn't keep up. Emerson then asked Philip Heuisler, an executive of his company, to do some problem solving. Heuisler organized the Maryland Glass Company, which began to manufacture a squatty little bottle of vivid cobalt blue shaped like R2-D2, the *Star Wars* robot. Each bottle held 3 teaspoons -- a single dose. It settled the nerves and did wonders for a hangover.

Later on, a Dr. Bunting with a pharmacy on Baltimore's North Avenue, developed Noxzema cream to protect sunbathers from burning and Mr. Heuisler sold him on the idea of using blue glass jars for his cream.   Early Noxzema jars had a pleasing 8-sided design. A whole generation of sunbathers identified the smell of Noxzema with summer. Then Vick's Vapo-Rub came along, also demanding a blue glass bottle. One sniff of "Vick's Salve" can carry you back to childhood, home and mother.

Most of this information I got from Joe Browne who spun it off the top of his head, spelling Heuisler properly without even checking. And at that time, although his health was failing, his mind and memory were young.

A day later, he called back with gossip about Col. Emerson's personal life he thought I might enjoy knowing. Baltimore was his turf and he knew every inch of it.

Joe Browne had a rare gift for friendship. He set you at ease. He listened and when he spoke, his words related to your thought. It was simple -- he liked people, all sorts of people. He liked to take his Taylor's Island neighbors to Baltimore for an Orioles baseball game. He went hunting with them and the following week invited his banker friends from Baltimore to come down for some quail shooting. He was never pompous, never self-important. Impatient, yes. Unforgiving, no.

He stripped down what he had to say to essentials. As a result I remember things he told me years ago. Like how he began his banking career as a young boy with good penmanship. It never left him. Typewriters and word processors were not for Joe Browne. He would write forcefully and briefly in longhand on a yellow pad.

Though he liked to reminisce, he was never long winded, never a bore, because he was selective and his touch was light. Joe Browne made you feel good. As for me, he gave me confidence; he never patronized. He was a fair and unsparing critic so that when he said "Well done," you knew you *had* done well.

He left Elizabeth a widow not long after I lost Joe Kolarek.

Living Alone

Joseph C. Kolarek, born June 18, 1915, died April 11, 1987, lies in Old Trinity Church yard beside the waters of a gentle stream called Church Creek. We had wandered through this cemetery while we were still new to the Eastern Shore and agreed it would be the perfect place to spend eternity. Joe had been diagnosed with lung cancer, and as he lay mortally ill in the hospital I asked his priest to visit him frequently. Joe was a faithful member of Father Eckrich's flock at St. Mary's Refuge of Sinners Church in Cambridge and a contributor to his many projects, like repairing the leaky roof of the Minette Dick Hall beside the church. The priest was an innovative fund raiser. Appeals were always headed with the names of two generous contributors -- Catherine Claws and Bob Barker, his cat and his dog.

Asking Father Joe to visit the Cambridge hospital was asking for a big favor. A construction project was under way and the streets around the hospital were so torn up that getting into the parking lot was like threading through a maze. One day half the streets were one-way. The next day they were altogether closed. Every day visitors were offered a new obstacle to overcome.

One afternoon when I arrived Joe told me that Father Eckrich had just left and had promised Joe that he would roll straight out of the Cambridge Hospital into Heaven.

"Really?" I said. "And did Father Eckrich also tell you that they have just torn Hell out of the streets leading to the highway?" Joe, somewhat sedated, needed a minute to take this in. Then he laughed, he roared, and I laughed with him. It was our last laugh together.

Halloween

During the fifteen Octobers we spent on Taylor's Island, never once did trick-or-treaters come to our door.   On an autumn evening with strands of mist rising from the water around us, with a spark or two of St. Elmo's fire skittering across the marsh, with acres of dry soy bean pods rustling and rattling in the breeze -- who would venture two miles down an unlighted road to rouse the occupants of a house at least 150 years old for a handful of candy? I doubt Stephen King would have come knocking.

Nothing could have been more benign under a sunny sky than this well- established old house with its pier reaching out into the water and its honeysuckle hedge that bloomed so sweetly in the summer.   But on Halloween night the imagination took charge. Lights shone spookily from attic windows and ghosts and goblins hid in the darkness, malice in their hearts.

Although I was now alone in the house, I was at ease and comfortable. When dark fell, spring, summer, winter or fall, I would let the two dogs out and we would walk over to the pond, about a city block away.

This small body of water, not quite half an acre in size, had been dug for us by a local gentleman with a piece of equipment called a drag line. We called it the "Pawn" in honor of his pronunciation of the word.

Our backs to the house, the dogs and I walked into total darkness. On nights when the stars were brilliant in a cloudless sky we walked by starlight. We walked around the pond and if the dogs chased off after some small creature rustling in the grass, I stood in the darkness and waited, quiet, at peace.

On still nights when the air was icy and the owl in the woods called his soft "Whooo," I wondered if "for all his feathers he was a-cold."   Sometimes a thin coat of ice formed over the water in the pond, scarcely thick enough to keep the reflection of the gibbous moon from sinking into the depths. My breath and the dogs' floated away as vapor.   I loved to walk around the pond on such a night, loved the feeling of being completely alone in the world with only moonlight for company. I knew that warmth and light waited inside the house when I turned and headed home, whistling up the dogs. They would be waiting at the door, cold and happy, and scamper inside ahead of me.

Nothing ever happened to disturb my peace of mind on these walks. I looked forward to them as punctuation marks at end the day. When we came inside, I never locked the doors. Many of my friends who had been born and raised on the Island thought it strange that I should choose such a way of life. They would never live way out there, all alone, they said. Too scary.

Wet Woods in Winter
February 2, 1990

Mother Nature has done a fine job of pruning her woods on Taylor's Island this past winter. First, we had a heavy, wet snow that bowed branches to the very ground. Then temperatures fell drastically, well below normal. I have noticed that cold snaps, when the temperature takes a sudden downturn, make even living wood brittle.

Then violent winds came up and blew the brittle branches from the weakened trees. They litter the forest floor. By summer they will have been invaded by wood-boring insects, become covered over with brambles and honeysuckle and be hidden from sight. Winter's surgical scars covered by summer's cosmetics.

For every fallen giant, dozens of young pines and cedars have popped up. Young hollies abound in clumps of 20 or more trees.

The two dogs wander and sniff happily, running crazy patterns through the woods, always keeping each other in view, and conscious at the same time of my whereabouts. Mitzi now leaps over the narrow ditches without hesitation. I no longer have to encourage her with "Jump, Mitzi, jump! You can do it." Boomer sails over all of them, no matter how wide, how deeply filled with water.

Today it is wet -- not a day with rain pouring down, but a day when the rain has stopped, the air is sodden and the woods are soaked. This is the perfect time for a walk.

Colors have changed. The moss and lichen which cover the trunks of old trees has turned a soft, velvety grey-green. The stark black trunks of the young pines stand out sharply against the ruddy pine needles that carpet the floor of the woods.

On a sunny day you do not see these things. On a sunny day in winter, it is apt to be chilly. A nippy wind discourages lingering and admiring. But when the temperature stands around 50 degrees you can indulge yourself. You can notice places where the woods are so dense that you can imagine the pine-covered woodland extends all the way to the banks of the

Mississippi River.   Then, after a bend in the road, the clear light sifts through.

The briars form barriers, knitting themselves to the lower branches of young trees, growing denser and denser each year. Beyond just such a thicket lay the Sleeping Beauty, as the Brothers Grimm wrote, waiting for the Prince to awaken her with a kiss. One hundred years of waiting, and these fairy tale princesses are still young and fresh and beautiful, untouched by time.   Did the Brothers Grimm know a secret?   Were they telling us that no matter how old a woman may be, the kiss of love will awaken her, enliven her, rejuvenate her?

New Year's Day, 1991.
Locked Out

The west wind had an uncanny knack for finding the tiniest crack to come through, whistling as it went. In winter, the wind comes out of the west with gale force. It can defeat the best heating system money can buy, as temperatures plummet. Consequently, we learned how to batten down the western side of the house with heavy plywood pieces cut to fit the door openings, backed up with double batts of insulation and screwed into place. I personally caulked around the edges, sealing up any miniscule openings as tightly as possible.

That job finished, we reminded ourselves to never get locked out in the wintertime.

It was New Year's Day, and iron cold. As I followed the dogs out the kitchen door and slammed it behind me I heard the fateful click of the old-fashioned thumb latch slipping into place.   I was locked out.

When that happened in the summer I could always walk in through another door. This time, I could not. The screen porch was securely wrapped in a layer of heavy insulating plastic. The two west doors were battened down. This time I was truly locked out.

Fortunately, I had made it an inflexible rule to leave an ignition key in of one of the cars, and after walking around the house a couple of times, just to be sure there really was no way in, I drove off for help. The dogs halfheartedly chased me down the lane, but found another scent and raced across the field.

I went straight to David and Anita Sears' house and found David in. He picked up a screwdriver, a chisel and some other tools and followed me home in his truck. He was able to remove one of the panels, patiently taking out a dozen screws, and we opened the door to the living room.

Back inside, in the warmth, I was overcome with the feeling that this time I had been lucky. What about next time --

the next unforeseen crisis? The next small, unanticipated mishap? Power failures sometimes left me without light or warmth. Pipes could freeze -- as they had done spectacularly one Christmas. No, I told myself. Face it. This solitary life places me in jeopardy.

As David put the insulated panel back in place he told me that he and Anita were concerned about my welfare. And I had often heard my neighbors say, winter and summer, "I wouldn't live way down there all by myself. Not me. Never."

I walked with David to the lane and we stood by the leafless fig tree stamping our feet on the hard ground.

"It's time to leave, isn't it?" I said. He was silent for a while. Then he said.

"Just don't move away and leave the place empty."

"No," I agreed. "I'd have to sell it."

And he got in his old green pickup truck with the rusty spot under the passenger door and headed down the lane.

I went inside and cried.

Goodbye
August 1991

It was a summer afternoon to remember. A group of youngsters was crabbing from the pier as a parent or two hovered nearby. Chicken necks dangled from long strings into the water. The crabbers stood with nets at the ready, waiting for a crab to take the bait.

Their voices floated up to the screened porch where I sat with the Sunday comics.

"Look, look. There's a big one."

"Careful. Be careful. Ah, Petie, you let him get away, you dummy."

"Shhhh. Bob's got a real biggie."

"Slow, slow now. Bring him up. Okay. Good. I got him."

"Oh, wow. He's BIG. How many we got now?"

And splitting this litany, there came a piercing scream.

My niece flew toward the house.

"Aunt Fran. Aunt Fran. It's a snake. There's a snake down there. Come quick."

Crabbing was abandoned. The group had formed a little circle around the snake, keeping a safe distance. There was tension and fear, born of their uncertainty about what to do. City folks have no experience with snakes. One of the boys offered to kill him.

"Want me to kill 'im, Aunt Fran?" There is ever the need to play the hero.

I took a quick look and said:

"Oh. That's Henry."

And the tension collapsed the way a chewing gum bubble breaks on a little boy's face.

"He's YOUR snake?" someone asked.

"Not exactly mine," I explained. "But we both live here."

At that moment Mitzi, the miniature Schnauzer, bolted through the screen porch door, trotted across the grass, jumped over the snake as if it did not exist, and sped toward the pier

177

where the chicken necks lay unguarded. As if the dog's shadow had erased the snake, the crabbers raced to rescue their bait.

I stood looking at Henry, about three feet long, black and glossy. He had just finished shedding. Exhausted, he lay in the sunny grass making his recovery. I felt sorry for him. His body had the spiral configuration a black snake takes while shedding. He looked so defenseless.

Shedding is hard work. I often found snake sheds, one corner wedged in a crack to anchor the old skin while the snake struggled to free himself. I had read once that sometimes very large crabs die in the process of molting, finding the old shell holding too fast, finding the effort too great.

In these abandoned snake sheds I had found a lesson I tried to use in my own life. Every year the snake leaves his old skin, struggles away from his former self, and become a new-born creature. He doesn't look back; just catches his breath, as Henry was doing, smoothes the wrinkles from his new person and moves along.

I knew this crabbing party would be the last one from my pier. I knew I was shedding this happy, comfortable country life for another new life, leaving the old skin behind.

And I hoped I could do it with the grace and dignity of Henry.

Yesterday's Embers
January, 2000

The chair in my kitchen is an ugly old relic.   It came out of a factory around 1920 and was probably sold in Sears Roebuck catalogues for 50 cents. Along with five other similar, but not identical, chairs, it waited forlornly at the kitchen table the day in 1960 when we moved into the house.

When I first saw these chairs they had all been covered with a thick coat of white paint, now soiled.   The original brown varnish showed through where the paint had cracked. Some of the seats had been covered with a black leatherette and excelsior stuffing had worked its way out through the odd crack.

We did not particularly notice these flaws as we sat down to our first meal in the old kitchen, happy to look out at the creek and listen to the birds complaining about our invasion of their privacy.

As I was leaving Taylor's Island, drastically paring down possessions, ruthlessly throwing things away, I went down to the barn where we stored old junk, and hauled out this chair.   I had the paint removed, like you would take a wash rag to the face of a scruffy orphan and then gave it a fresh new coat of white paint, not motivated by any sense that it might have value.

I expect I did it for the same reason we never replaced the wooden spools that served as door pulls on the old screen doors.

For the same reason we never touched the patch on the door between the great room and kitchen.

For the same reason I keep old bottles lined up on a kitchen shelf above this ugly old chair.   Since these objects have neither beauty nor value, it would seem that I have appointed myself curator of worthless things.

Call it an atavism. Say that I still fear that tomorrow's fire will die if I do not tend yesterday's embers.

2473691

Made in the USA